Lies Start-Ups Tell Themselves to Avoid Marketing

Lies Start-Ups Tell Themselves to Avoid Marketing

A No Bullsh*t Guide for Ph.D.s, Lab Rats, Suits, and Entrepreneurs

Sandra Holtzman and Jean Kondek

SelectBooks, Inc.
New York

First Edition

ISBN-10: 1-59079-107-X
ISBN-13: 978-1-59079-107-3

Library of Congress Cataloging-in-Publication Data

Holtzman, Sandra, 1951–

Lies start-ups tell themselves to avoid marketing : a no bull-** guide for Ph.D.s, lab rats, suits and garage inventors / by Sandra Holtzman and Jean Kondek. -- 1st ed.

p. cm.

Includes bibliographical references.

ISBN-13: 978-1-59079-107-3 (pbk. : alk. paper)
ISBN-10: 1-59079-107-X

1. Marketing. 2. New business enterprises. I. Kondek, Jean, 1940–
II. Title.

HF5415.H725 2007
658.8--dc22

2006037116

Manufactured in the United States of America
10 9 8 7 6 5 4 3 2 1

Dedicated to Gene Guberman

For his profound, intuitive, and amazing understanding of human behavior and for his generous sharing of that knowledge with me. I have learned from him that all business is based on relationships between people—when the relationships function well, business succeeds. When they don't, business struggles.

Sandra Holtzman

Dedicated to David Leddick

For seeing a spark in me no one else saw, least of all myself, and for introducing me to the outrageous world of advertising. And to all the outstanding men and women I've met in this crazed business. You're the ones who have taught me that skillful communications can change the course of business, people and quite possibly the world.

Jean Ross Kondek

Contents

	Foreword	ix
	How to Use This Book	xi
Lie #1	If I Build It, They Will Come.	1
Lie #2	There Is No Point in Promoting My Product Until It's Completely Ready.	14
Lie #3	I Don't Have to Market Now Since I Have Better Science Than the Big Guys. Or, My Ideas Will Be Stolen If I Market.	27
Lie #4	I Have to Show a Profit Before I Can Market.	33
Lie #5	I Only Need a Web Site.	39
Lie #6	I Need to Do Public Relations First.	61
Lie #7	I Know How to Market.	73
Lie #8	I Have a Business Plan; I Don't Need a Marketing Plan.	77
Lie #9	Only a Technical Person Can Market My Product.	91
Lie #10	I Can Get the Work Done Cheaper.	97
	No More Lies	107
	Biographies of Those Quoted	109
	About the Authors	113

Foreword

Working as a marketer in the biotechnology and IT markets, I have heard it all. One business founder after another always seems to have some reason why they do not need to market their company, product, or service "yet." There is always some rationale not to promote their new venture. These people just don't get it.

One night over dinner, after working hard on yet another new marketing campaign, Sandy Holtzman and I began to compare notes about how frustrating it is to work with entrepreneurs who seem to miss one key ingredient needed for their success: marketing. Though they have creative ideas for a new product or service, they are afraid to communicate their exciting new company to others. After dessert, and just for fun, we grabbed a pen and a napkin and began to create a list of all the excuses we had heard. We laughed hard that night, but the next day we realized we had created a useful list that might help these creative people see how they are missing out on something that could make them a success. That is how the idea for this book began.

By chance, within weeks, I had an opportunity to give a presentation to a local business organization in Cincinnati. I called Sandy and said I would like to use our list of excuses, which we changed into lies, for my talk. After we'd compared notes and created the presentation together, the idea of turning this concept into a useful book for entrepreneurs became real.

Not long afterward, Sandy was talking to Jean Kondek, whose background was in consumer and business-to-business (B2B) marketing on Madison Avenue and in smaller, regional agencies. Her experiences in working with start-ups paralleled ours. It seems the issues and attitudes that bedevil entrepreneurs are common to all regardless of business category or depth of funding.

About that time, I had the opportunity to work at Hill Top, and the demands on my time prevented me from pursuing the book. Sandy took it on and brought in Jean. The result of their collective wisdom is in your hands.

I have worked with Sandy Holtzman for many years marketing biotech and IT companies. She has had her own marketing and advertising company for nine years and has focused on serving pharma, biotech, and high-tech businesses. Jean Kondek has worked on high-tech start-ups as well as a full range of B2B and consumer businesses.

Through all these experiences, they have honed their skills helping business founders market their companies. Their depth of experience can help all entrepreneurs overcome all excuses not to market their companies right away. If even one entrepreneur who reads this book begins to promote his or her company right away, all the efforts in putting this book together will be worthwhile.

Joel Ivers
CEO, Hill Top Research Corporation

How to Use this Book

This book is based on our experiences in marketing all kinds of products. Some of our experiences led to great rewards. Some led to long days and nights of pizza, coffee, and antacids as we struggled to create work that would deliver more than our clients had imagined.

Like most experiences, this book is non-linear, and the chapters don't build sequentially. Pick the Lie that resonates with you and start reading there. Each chapter is complete and actionable.

Use this book as your toolbox of ideas and guidelines, as a reference book, as a road map, or as just a good read. Regardless of how you approach the information, it is going to help you focus on taking your wonderful concept, company, product, division, or service to success sooner rather than later with less need for antacids.

We have gone out of our way to make it a common sense collection of what you need to know to launch your baby. We have deliberately left out the usual jargon, gobbledygook, and malarkey (what we call smoke and mirrors in the ad business) that has grown up around marketing. It's not rocket science, but it is hard work. It needs focus, attention to detail, and the use of best practices. We know you're up to it. And we're happy to hold your hand all the way.

Lie #1 ·

If I Build It,
They Will Come

"First, create value. Next identify the highest probability customers. Finally, find the most cost-effective (with the emphasis on 'effective') way to get your message across."

Marv Goldschmitt,
Serial entrepreneur who launched 1-2-3 for Lotus

Let's talk about this. Even if your product, concept, or idea is wonderful, how can you be sure they will buy it?

Of course they will, you say. "I'm a scientist, I know. This is great science. This is going to make everyone's life easier. It's a unique solution that's going to save time, money, and resources."

Let's say that's all true. How will your prospective buyers learn about the existence of your product?

We need to be clear here. Lab researchers, CEOs, and other decision makers are not sitting around waiting for your product to show up. They're too busy solving problems with the technology they have today. They may be eager to use your product once they know about it, but how will they learn about it? This is the critical problem that marketing solves. It's true for every new product or service, whether it's intended for the scientist in the lab or the average working Joe.

Another critical issue is timing. If your ideal customer is a company, how fast will it be able to set aside a budget to purchase your product? And how long is its approval process for purchasing? Your ideal purchaser may be a company whose budgets are approved based on spending plans submitted about a year in advance. Are you prepared to wait? Can you *afford* to wait?

Do your marketing homework, and you shouldn't need to wait at all. This applies to any product or service.

TRUTH #1:

You aren't waiting for someone else's product, so why should they be waiting for yours?

Until you lay the marketing groundwork for your product's introduction (the "launch," as it's called in the communications business), no one will know it's there. It is important to understand the process of marketing—and the purchasing process of your potential customers—even though both may be outside your area of expertise.

Here's an example: You take vitamins. One day at the store you notice that among the products from familiar names—Twin Labs, Kal, Solgar, the house brand—there's a new brand of vitamin. You read the label and see that it has better ingredients. But you've never heard of the brand and know nothing about the company. So, though you've been exposed to a product that sounds a lot better, you buy the same old thing. There's a simple reason for this: You weren't prepared for it. You know nothing about the vitamin or company that makes it, it hasn't been recommended in any way, no one you know uses it, you haven't read or seen ads about it, and it may even cost more. It's sitting on the shelf, and that's what happens if you "build it" but don't prepare the purchasing environment. The product just sits there. That is, if you're lucky enough to get a distributor or retailer to carry it.

Though this example is from consumer marketing, the same scenario happens in any marketing environment.

It's true even if you're building a unique science that will increase the number of XYZ molecules, making them cheaper and of a higher quality (more pure) than anything available. It's equally true if you're opening a new candy store. Your entry into the marketplace has to be announced. Awareness and credibility need to be established to reach profitability as quickly as possible.

So, what have you done to build awareness and credibility for your product or business?

How are you going to reach out to your customers? Do you know who all your potential customers are? *Really?* If you're selling directly to your customer, how many sales calls do you think it takes to get one appointment? How many appointments do you think it takes to get one sale?

Let's put it another way. How many blind vendor calls do *you* accept each day? Maybe you're going to write your prospects a letter of introduction. How much unsolicited mail do *you* get each day? How much of it do you pay attention to?

Maybe you're going to network at trade shows. How much time do you have to play hit and miss with the 200 business cards you will surely collect? More importantly, where is the best place to put your energy? Aren't you more valuable managing your business and doing what only you can do to grow and enhance your company's value?

Let's face it: Your value to your company is in your head, not in selling your product and your business, one phone call, one business card, one letter at a time.

CRITICAL TAKEAWAY: Even if you've been talking up your product or idea for years, the purchasing environment that needs to be developed has not yet been created. That's what marketing does. It creates a desire or pressure to fulfill an existing need for a product like yours. It articulates the need for your product. This, in turn, initiates a whole chain of events focused on purchasing your product to fulfill that need.

LESSON #1:

Building Your Market—The Adopter Pyramid

It's time to understand the dynamics of the arena you are about to enter. Not all of your customers think alike or have the same mindset. The Adopter pyramid (shown here) depicts the different mindsets that exist in your market and how they relate to each other. It helps to explain why not everyone in your market will be interested in your product for the same reason or at the same time even if they need it.

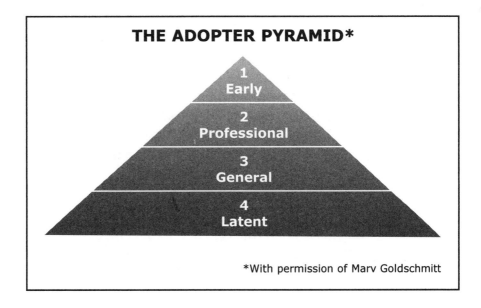

THE ADOPTER PYRAMID*

1 Early

2 Professional

3 General

4 Latent

*With permission of Marv Goldschmitt

Early Adopters

At the top of the pyramid is the critical group of people who will be immediately attuned to your product and willing to purchase or use it immediately. We call these people Early Adopters.

In the consumer world, they are often the first people on your block with the latest gadget. They can't wait to show it to you and explain how it works. You may even call on these neighborhood experts when you are ready to purchase new technology. You rely on them to tell you what brand to buy, where to get it, how to assemble it, and so on.

This scenario is equally true in the scientific/technology community.

Early Adopters are continually searching for new and sexy technologies to use in their own work. When they take an interest in your technology, they give it immediate credibility. They have the ears of others who might be interested in new technologies, such as corporate CEOs and investors. Because they are seen as authorities, they often can obtain the funding needed to purchase and integrate your technology into their existing processes. In this way, they help you build your product's credibility as they help you build your market.

An added bonus is that Early Adopters frequently find new applications or reasons for your product you never considered, and they can find the financing to develop those new applications. Reaching the Early Adopters is the first and most economical step to reaching people who will give you credibility, providing evidence that your idea or product works in the real world.

Every product or service has its Early Adopters. You see them when a trendy new restaurant opens. You see them when hybrid cars are introduced. And they're visible when new fashions are for sale.

The pyramid shows that Early Adopters are the smallest market. They are, therefore, the most economical to reach. Like the guy in your neighborhood with all the latest gadgets, they are willing to take the risk with something new. In short, they become the authorities, the trend-setters that introduce your product and its applications to the next group of Adopters.

We call this next group the Professional Adopters.

Professional Adopters

Professional Adopters are equally capable of understanding your product and are always looking for a competitive advantage. They communicate with Early Adopters on a regular basis, hunting for news and information on the latest thing in their area of interest.

Professional Adopters actually seek out Early Adopters, who then influence them to follow their lead.

So, after the Early Adopters, the Professional Adopters are the most likely to pick up your product and use it. However, this second tier of users is larger, which means you'll need to spend more to reach and convert them from their existing technology solutions.

Professional Adopters represent a wider base of potential users and influencers. If yours is a technology or business product, Professional Adopters are more likely to adopt it across departments and whole corporations. This is the market from which you are likely to see your first significant profits. The same is true for consumer products. It represents the point at which your product or business enters the mainstream and begins achieving legitimacy.

This legitimacy now makes it OK for the third group of Adopters to step up to the counter.

General Adopters

We call this third group General Adopters. They tend to be much more cautious about new trends. They may have significant budget constraints, which encourage them to have a "wait and see" attitude, especially toward new technologies. No one in this group wants to recommend a new technology that might fail, cost their company money, and perhaps cost them their job. Nor do they want to recommend a restaurant or fashion item that hasn't been fully proven by others. They depend on the Professional Adopters for information on proven new trends.

By the time General Adopters pick up your technology, it will have a few gray hairs on it. However, they are a very large market. In most cases this is the market that will generate your most significant revenues. Think of them as your general use market.

They, in turn, influence the Latent Adopter market.

Latent Adopters

Latent Adopters adopt your idea long after it has become the standard. In fact, this group often adopts it after the Early Adopters have thrown it out. Latent Adopters are a mixed bag. If businesses are your customers, Latent Adopters can be large, slow-moving companies, start-ups with small budgets, or new under-funded divisions. In the case of consumers, they can be those who hate change, have less to spend, or only buy when forced.

The plus side? Latent Adopters are a larger market, and when they buy, they buy in volume. The minus side? You have to stay in business long enough for them to catch up. If you're a typical entrepreneur you may not even own the company anymore by the time these guys buy. (You may want to make provisions for them in your exit strategy.).

Strategizing Your Market

So, let's sum up.

The most economical way to begin selling your product is to start with the Early Adopters. They are the smallest group, so your message can be more focused. They have a similar mindset to yours, and they'll look at your product or business and understand the need it fulfills immediately.

Early Adopters are the most influential group on the pyramid. Reaching them requires the least amount of money and time; however, you'll have to be innovative in getting your message to them because they are not found in traditional trade and business venues.

You can't lie or over-promise to Early Adopters. If your product has problems, you must address them. Early Adopters almost always work around problems, which is especially true in technology where they expect to find bugs. If your product has drawbacks, own up to them. If you don't, rest assured someone will find them, and the result will be bad publicity. Remember that all segments of your market will speak to each other and find out the truth.

Even with kinks, your product needs to deliver the first time out. If it doesn't, you will have lost a significant opportunity, since this same group of positive influencers can influence others negatively. This group is not concerned about risk. They are willing to hear an exciting message, and they are driven to find new technologies that pique their interest with little regard for return on investment (ROI), profitability, or risk.

The next most economical group to reach is Professional Adopters.

You need a sexy message for them. This audience *is* concerned with ROI, profitability, and risk. Because Professional Adopters are a larger group than Early Adopters, they will cost more to reach, and your message will have to be seen in more venues. You will face more competition from others wanting to reach the same audience. Likewise, they will have more demands on their time, attention, budget, etc.

By the time you get to the General Adopters, your product should have a track record and be less risky to adopt.

Now, your sexy message needs more. It needs to have "permission to believe" added to it in the form of usage examples by respected groups like the Professional Adopters. And you have to turn up the volume of your message to break through the marketplace clutter. This entails more expense. You have to fight this audience's inertia and its resistance to change. They will often agree with you that your product is great and yet still resist.

Competitors will become a significant factor. They may have entered your marketplace with "me-too" products, so your marketing efforts will need to be more intense to make your product stand out from the clutter caused by the competition. Here, your product is the most vulnerable because the competition can take over the whole market. You have paved the way for them to do that by being first.

However, most of your profit will come from the General Adopters. It's also the group with the most resistance to your sales message, since they are already financially, emotionally, and politically invested in existing technologies.

Now we come to the Latent Adopters.

By the time they purchase your product, they are so far behind the curve that they have to buy it just to keep up with the industry. They have the most inertia. Though the risk factor for your product has virtually disappeared, this group is driven by a different kind of risk: the risk of being left behind and not being able to utilize new technologies. Think of it as not upgrading your computer often enough. Suddenly, you can't interface with others as you used to.

CRITICAL TAKEAWAY: Though all of these markets speak to and influence each other, they do not do this in a vacuum. You must constantly be sending your message into the pyramid to reinforce what they are hearing on the inside.

A Note of Caution for Being First

The sad fact is that being first to market does not necessarily mean you will win the market. There's a saying, "First to market, first to fail." Apple's Newton is a perfect example of this theory.

First developed to be a new form of personal computing, the Newton offered handwriting recognition, a notepad for input, a new way of programming, and a new kind of operating system in one handheld device. As with many innovations, all of its advances offered their own set of problems that programmers and users had to overcome. Nevertheless, it was unique, and it opened up a category that would be called the Personal Digital Assistant (PDA). The Newton was introduced in proper order to Early Adopters who talked it up. And it was supported by all the marketing drama we have come to expect from an Apple product launch. Yet in spite of its revolutionary nature and all the buzz surrounding it, the Newton failed to grab hold.

Though many reasons existed for the failure, three were most critical. The Newton's cost was too high for its market. Though it was a handheld device, it failed the "pocket test" (it didn't fit into the user's pocket). Most importantly, the Newton's handwriting recognition did not live up to its hype.

User disappointment was massive. By the time Newton OS2, the second version, came out with improved handwriting recognition as well as plenty of new bells and whistles, the die had been cast. The product could not overcome the negativity generated by the first version. It was, however, a success in that it opened up a new niche in personal computing that would soon be filled by Palm, Inc.'s PDA, the Palm Pilot.

This newer PDA learned from the mistakes of the Newton, with an improved handwriting recognition system, lower cost, and smaller size. Today, PDAs are everywhere. Everyone knows someone with a Blackberry. Manufacturers are creating newer devices almost by the hour. Will nano computers trump cell phones by becoming the next cool PDA, or will they all converge and evolve into something more novel?

Who knows? Our point is that being first, unique, and the hottest, sexiest, most exciting thing to come down the pike in years still does not guarantee success. Expectations for a new technology need to be managed. If users must change their behaviors, they will need to be supported in doing so. If pricing puts the product beyond the reach of its market, product adjustments have to be made. All these marketing concerns need to be addressed well in advance for a successful launch.

Apple's iPod has the reverse story. It did address user concerns for ease of use, capacity, size, access to music, cost, and "coolness," and it immediately took over the MP3 market. Though it was not the first MP3 player, this foresight combined with "hot" commercials, iPod storefronts, and great product placements branded it as the player of choice. Regular enhancements and an array of peripherals continue to solidify its hold on the market.

Case History: Texas Instruments™ Semiconductor Product

New products and technologies can often be introduced to Early Adopters simply, inexpensively, and effectively by using venues outside traditional media. Trade newsletters and blogs are two possibilities.

Here is an example of a product being "advertised" in an unglamorous way, at least by traditional standards. However, the venue is frequented by Texas Instrument's (TI) target market, electrical and electronic engineers who are Early Adopters. This is an example of a classified announcement type of ad posted on a web site called E1394™ Trade Association. (The E1394™ Trade Association supports the development of electronics systems that can be easily connected with each other using a single serial multimedia link.)

TI developed the semiconductor, TSB12LV21B. Since the name TI has significant brand recognition in the marketplace, someone browsing these pages will have certain assumptions about the technical capabilities of this product as well as the

assurance that the company will not go out of business and will stand behind the product. The people reading these pages will have a full understanding of the product. If you are looking for Early Adopters, this type of highly focused venue is a good place to go fishing.

Fancy advertising isn't needed at this stage because this product is not on the shelf, ready to sell to a mass market.

From the other end of the marketing spectrum is another example of a more complex company (still in start-up mode) with existing and potential customers in all of the pyramid segments.

Case History: Elumen Solutions

Elumen Solutions was a healthcare information technology company formed through the merger of two well-respected smaller companies, Exemplar Systems and Darca. Because of this merger and subsequent identity change, Elumen had to make a big splash in the marketplace immediately to:

- Continue an aggressive growth goal
- Establish itself as a major player in its sector
- Maintain the customer bases of the two original companies
- Announce that the newer and larger company had more services to offer
- Attract attention of customers, venture capitalists, industry analysts, potential partners, and buyers

Elumen had business relationships with all of the adopters in the pyramid and needed to announce the name change and reintroduce itself as a new entity offering more value. At the same time, it needed to reassure existing clients that the services it had previously provided and the people who had provided them would remain.

To do this, Elumen needed to convince the Early Adopters that it was still in the forefront, that it had more sexy stuff to offer, and that its company innovators would continue to innovate. Elumen needed to convince the Professional Adopters that it had more depth to the services it had offered. This meant that it could be called upon to handle bigger projects from start to finish. Additionally, the Early and Professional

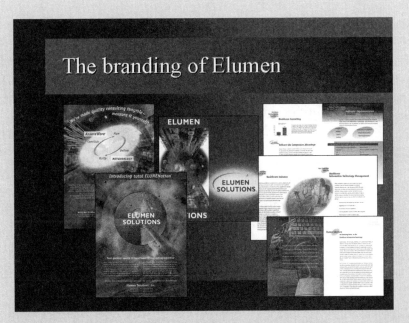

Adopters needed to be convinced that Elumen had newly proven methodologies that included more efficient, robust ways to produce results for its clients.

The General Adopters, being larger corporations, needed to be convinced that Elumen was proven and better equipped to handle larger assignments and that it had new methodologies and resources in place. The General Adopters needed to be convinced that Elumen could become a one-stop shop for companies dealing with multiple vendors who were delivering inconsistent results.

Latent Adopters had the same concerns as the General Adopter group. They had larger projects that may not have required the latest technology but did require maintenance of legacy systems and the migration of these systems into newer environments being installed.

These messages were conveyed in the work you see in the example above. This program allowed Elumen to speak to everyone in the Adopter Pyramid with a single voice. Within a year and a half, Elumen attracted the attention of a large multinational information technology consulting firm, which bought the company. It went from a $17 million company in its first year, to $60 million two years later, and to being sold for $89 million.

Elumen achieved this by creating an organized, well-thought-out marketing plan and program. The key factor in the success of this effort was consistency. It included consistent graphics, messaging, and delivery program that reached the entire pyramid. This process is called branding. As you dive deeper into the Adopter Pyramid and need to reach more people, branding becomes more critical. It separates you from the competition and keeps your product in the minds of potential purchasers.

If you are like most start-up companies, you probably face significant budget restrictions and can afford to reach only one segment of the pyramid. That segment should be the Early Adopters, the people best able to understand your product and communicate its value to others. By using smart branding tactics as Elumen did, you can dramatically increase the impact of your dollars.

As you can see, the materials exhibit a consistent graphic look that includes color palette, typefaces, and treatment of information. Individual pieces consisted of the following:

- A 12-page corporate brochure with a pocket in the back for additional information (to customize the materials for specific customer sales calls)
- One corporate umbrella ad
- Two product-specific ads
- Two four-page product-specific brochures
- Two product-specific direct mail pieces
- A trade show booth (incorporating the same graphics and messaging)

A web site detailing all technology services and products was also available.

A public relations effort was integrated with the marketing program and included the following:

- Six white papers describing the latest needs in the marketplace and how to address those needs technologically
- Magazine articles that were placed in relevant trade/industry journals
- Press releases to the trade press announcing new technology
- Press releases to the investment community and industry analysts to raise awareness of the company's growth
- Speaking engagements at major trade shows and investor conference calls for the CEO and senior staff and technology experts

Key elements of the message included Elumen's tag line (Using Our Intellectual Advantage™ to Your Competitive Advantage®), which appealed to all segments of the audience. "Intellectual Advantage" highlights Elumen's ability to do the following:

- Mobilize health care and information technology expertise
- Utilize proven methodologies
- Draw upon its corporate knowledge base to solve clients' business problems

This unique Intellectual Advantage allowed Elumen to support its clients by eliminating the need for multiple vendors and all the accompanying complexities. Elumen was able to deliver multiple high-end solutions from a single consulting source, which gave its clients a competitive edge in the marketplace.

Because this corporate messaging was open-ended, it accommodated the company's evolving needs and did not need to change as the company grew and launched new products. The consistent messaging supported the company as a long-term player while fostering trust in each new product.

So, If You Build It, Will They Come?

They probably won't. At least not in the numbers you will need to make a profit. And not rapidly enough to support your company, not even if you are one of those charismatic people able to enroll people in your product's idea. Your vision may make you an ideal person to rally the troops and lead the sales effort. Ultimately, though, successful marketing comes down to numbers. A marketing philosophy that has you waiting for the phone to ring will not generate the numbers needed for success.

On the other hand, having a great product is definitely a good start. It's always easier to build a marketing plan around an exciting concept that delivers a desirable benefit. So, they will come, but you'll just have to go out and get them.

Lie #2

There Is No Point in Promoting My Product Until It's Completely Ready

"If we waited to market each product until it was 100 percent ready, the company would be out of business before it started. In the IT world, often the first client generates the revenue to add the 'bells and whistles' to a product."

Susan A. Harsley,
Vice President of Marketing, MFX

If you're caught up in crossing every "t" and dotting every "I," then you're losing valuable time. Sales cycles for many products are long. A sales cycle is the length of time it will take you to reach customers and convince them of your product's value, added to the length of time it will take them to convince their company to buy it (or their husband, wife, child, parent, or anyone else who is involved in the purchasing decision).

Add this to the time it takes you to cross those t's, and you could be waiting a long time for those first payments to arrive. So, you need to ask yourself, "Can I afford to wait?" And how long can you hang on? What price are you willing to pay for perfection?

However, if you are only concerned about proving your concept, or making sure your product works correctly, then you are right to keep it under cover—*up to a point.*

If you know your technology or product still has kinks in it, a wiser choice might be to approach your market (individually or a small segment of it), and let potential customers know that it hasn't been fully vetted. Tell them you would welcome their input on this initial version. In the technology industry, this is called beta testing.

15

(For example, Voiceover Internet Protocol (VOIP) allows voice conversation over the internet. To induce people to try it, it was offered free during beta testing.) As part of this choice, you might offer your product at a discount or free in exchange for the client putting your ideas into action. This is a win-win situation for you and for your client.

If you wait until your product is finalized and then begin to market it, the first hurdle you will have to jump is your product's sales cycle. How you react to your product's sales cycle can make the difference between life and death for your company.

Make Sure Your Customers Love You as Much as Your Product

If you do send your unfinished baby out to potential clients, a crucial element of this endeavor will be your relationship to your customers, even if this means spending time and effort on issues indirectly related to your product's success. Keeping your customer happy is an important part of perfecting and selling your product and making your company successful.

Remember, these people are the gateway to your company's future success. If this area is uncomfortable for you, hire someone who can do it for you.

The Sales Cycle

A sales cycle is the time it takes from first meeting a potential customer until you close the deal. Depending on many factors, this could be one week, 18 months, or longer. When you add the time you need to research, find, and qualify that customer, you could be looking at months or years. Even if your product has a short sales cycle, you will need to factor in your marketing time, since it can reduce your cash flow and limit your operating expenses.

Anatomy of a Short Sales Cycle

If your product is as simple as an enzyme or lab kit, then a lab technician could read about it in a magazine, pick up the phone, and order the product. If you have an ad for a new kind of hair dryer, the same process applies. In each case, your sales cycle is only a few days. However, what seems like a simple, short sales cycle requires planning and forethought. To make that sale, you will already have handled a number of marketing chores.

If you're selling the lab kit, you'll have prepared protective packaging to hold and ship your test tube samples. You will have determined the volume of the samples in the kit and what price you must charge to make a profit. You will have written and printed a manual or instruction sheet on how to use the samples. You will have arranged for a customer service phone number and someone knowledgeable to answer it. Ideally, you'll have prepared packaging and communications materials with graphics and messaging that help brand your company and encourage your customer to come back for more.

Prior to making that sale, you will have done the research to identify your customers and how to reach them, what magazines they read, what meetings and shows they attend, where you can obtain a mailing list of qualified prospects, etc. Based on this information, you will have created an ad, web site, letter, or direct mail piece that introduces your product as the ideal solution for their problem. If you are running an ad, you will have made arrangements to place that ad in a magazine. This whole process can take several months and a lot of your valuable time.

Anatomy of a Long Sales Cycle

If yours is a more complex product or service, particularly one requiring a big corporate budget, you will probably be facing a long sales cycle. During this time, you will be meeting multiple decision makers throughout the client company, communicating with multiple departments, and dealing with various company procedures.

You will have to provide information about your company and your product and the stability of both to various levels at the client company. You will be expected to provide proof of concept and evidence of your product's benefits and reasons why you are better than the competition. You will need to prove that your company will be there after the sale to service the product, and that you will not go out of business after the client buys it.

As you go through the sales cycle, you will discover that different people within the client's company have different relationships to your product. With a more complex product—say, an electronic medical records product that must be adopted by a multi-physician medical practice—you may encounter three or four tiers or gatekeepers before getting a purchase approval. At each tier, you may find a different expert with a different agenda, a different investment in your product's adoption, and a different comfort level with your technology.

Physicians or medical staff may be concerned with the interface, ease of learning, speed, and how the product will help them better serve patients. The CFO or Practice Manager may be concerned about increased accuracy of reporting to insurance companies, compliance with the Heath Insurance Portability and Accountability Act (HIPAA), compatibility with current applications, cost savings, or payment issues. The technical buyer or CIO will be concerned with implementing the program, downtime, help desk functions, flexibility to add new features, training, and compatibility with suppliers, pharmacies, and hospitals.

A software product for a large company goes through a similar process and may take 18 months to two years or more to sell through. During this time, you will be talking to, and selling up through, the strata of your customer's company. This can include your customer's IT gatekeepers, the CFO, and the CEO. You will have to offer demos, proof of concept, and perhaps a free trial period. You may need to prove you can customize the product and handle integration seamlessly and that you can offer any necessary customer service after the product's installation. Moreover, you will need to prove the technology is compatible with the employees who will use it.

You will want to have proof that this type of technology is worthy of adoption and that yours is the one to buy. By preparing your message and marketing materials in advance of your launch, you will be ready for these challenges with any or all of the following:

- White papers
- Journal articles
- Actual or projected return on investment (ROI) information
- Software manuals
- References
- One or more existing, satisfied clients who will be willing to let you bring in a new client for a preview of how the system is performing in their business.

No matter what your product's sales cycle, here's the cold fact: It takes four to six months to begin to see the results of an advertising/marketing program once the program is launched. This does not take into account the length of time to prepare the program and create the materials.

For instance, if your product is going to be ready to sell next Monday, you need to have done your homework in advance and integrated your sales cycle with your promotion cycle so that both progress together. This makes more sense than waiting until Monday to start selling and promoting.

To Use or Not to Use A Marketing Agency?

Successful marketing requires work and time. At this point, you may want to consider bringing in an agency, an in-house marketing person, or both. These decisions will depend on your business plan, market characteristics, and product. The critical deciding factor, of course, will be your budget.

If you're going to market it yourself, you need to have several basics in place. You will have to decide on a strategy and write your marketing plan. The plan defines your market, where to find those in the market, and how to reach them. That means you will have decided which adopter segment(s) in your market you will go after, which means you will have done some research and discovered the best way(s) to reach them.

If you're going to use an advertising/marketing agency (which we recommend) to get the word out, decide on a budget as soon as possible. You should have some idea of what you can spend, because that's the first question the agency personnel will ask you.

If you have not considered your marketing budget, be prepared for a reality check when the agency people tell you what marketing costs. And do not faint when they tell you how much time the project is going to take.

You may change your mind and decide to do your marketing yourself, thinking you'll save money.

Suppose you want to launch at trade shows or professional meetings. You must ask yourself a series of strategic questions:

Do you know what trade shows you need to attend and your purpose for attending?

Are you going to do a pre-launch of your product, where the product is still in development but you want to get your company name and product concept out in the world to start building your market? Or will you do a proven-product launch, where you may have case histories and testimonials of the product in use?

Will you be an exhibitor at the trade show, or just attend and chat up your product to anyone you can? An exhibitor must consider a number of tactical details. You need to look at the floor plans and know which convention floor areas will give your booth the best exposure. You will probably need to sign up as an exhibitor six to twelve months in advance. You will have to find someone to design and produce your booth.

Having done all this preparation, you will be prepared to take advantage of all the opportunities the promoters offer, such as speaking opportunities, program ads, sponsorships for cocktail parties, hospitality suites at your hotel, and mailing lists of attendees (so you can send out postcard invitations to visit your booth). You will also have arranged for people from your company who are knowledgeable about the product, and who have a modicum of sales experience, to run the booth. You cannot and should not do this alone. You need to be available for impromptu and pre-arranged sales meetings.

Because you have notified potential customers that you will be at the show, they will have your booth number. More importantly, they will expect you to have something exciting to show them because you sent your postcard announcing your company's convention presence.

This example shows that successful marketing requires thinking, planning, and timing before the product launch. If you wait until your product is finalized, it will be several months before you will be prepared to introduce it. Moreover, the longer your projected sales cycle, the more critical it is to initiate your marketing efforts in advance of product launch.

We have covered the surface tactics to give you an idea of the details involved in attending even a simple trade show. You will need to determine if you will perform all this work yourself—including sourcing suppliers such as printers, convention booth manufacturers, and shippers—will have an in-house person do it, such as a marketing director or marketing manager, or will hand it off to a marketing agency.

TRUTH #2:

You need to build your market while you are building your product. Perfecting your product is an inward-looking process. Preparing and initiating your sales and marketing effort is an outward-looking process. They are both active, and they need to occur simultaneously. That way you'll have prepared your market to buy your product and will have minimized the delay in starting your revenue stream.

A wonderful example of this is how Apple Computer generates huge excitement for its new products long before it launches them. By launch date, Early Adopters are ready to snap up the latest product. They know what the new computer's capabilities are, and they want it because Apple has prepared the purchasing environment and has articulated the need for the product and, thus, the desire to own it.

You are not Apple, but the same sales and promotion cycle concept applies to every company no matter what its size or the product type. So, what is the most efficient way to build the need for your product while you are building the product? The most effective marketing programs begin with the development of a branding position.

LESSON #2:

Building Your Brand While You Build Your Product

What is branding? And what does it do?

Books have been written about branding. The business world is filled with branding gurus. Though branding is the buzzword at every convention of marketing professionals, it is as old as the hills. P. T. Barnum knew what it was and how to use it. IBM built a brand known for quality in business machines for decades. Charles Revson started with nail polish and built an international cosmetic and healthcare empire using astute branding. Branding is the reason we make a Xerox instead of a copy. It's why we ask for Kleenex instead of tissues, and it's why every brand of string trimmer is called a Weed Whacker.

Branding enables a company to differentiate itself from the competition. It is an intangible and emotional response by the customer to your marketing materials, leading to a sense of loyalty. This loyalty grows as your product lives up to its promises and the customer continues to be exposed to your messages. The emotional connection makes it difficult for the competition to intrude.

> **Branding: It's Not What You Say; It's What They Take Away**
>
> People will always have opinions, feelings, and judgments about your product. Your branding is how you mold these reactions in your favor.

Branding creates a bond that goes beyond product satisfaction. It is the reason people feel more secure with name-brand medications even when generics offer cheaper, equally efficacious alternatives. Branding is the basis, or bottom line, of all effective marketing. A well-branded company that occasionally makes a mistake and produces a poor product will be forgiven. A poor product without a branded foundation can kill a company.

In short, branding has the following impact:

- Branding is what's left in your customer's mind after your marketing goes away.
- Branding carries over from one product to another.
- Branding builds trust and loyalty, which combat cheaper, "me-too" products and services that may want to ride on your coattails.

Branding: The Basics

1. Branding differentiates your company from the competition.

This is especially critical for a start-up company. Branding enables you to create a niche for your company or product in the marketplace. It separates a company or product from the pack and enables customers to remember your unique message. For instance, Nike stands for "Just do it." With the increased interest in healthy eating, the pork industry has repositioned itself as "Pork—the other white meat."

2. Branding creates a unique company identity and personality.

This personality will be reflected in all your communications materials as well as in how people perceive your company. It will be reflected in your logo or mark and in your tag line or commanding claim. It will be reflected in everything you do: how you speak about yourself and how people—customers, the press, industry analysts, experts—think about you and refer to you in public. When people hear your name or see any representation of your company, product, or technology, they will know who you are and what you stand for.

For instance, BASF, which makes numerous ingredients that go into enhancing other products, shows the public how extensive its contribution is with its line: "We don't make the [product], we make it better." The *New York Times* takes its positioning line seriously— "All the news that's fit to print"—making it the go-to newspaper for in-depth reporting.

3. *Branding is a representation of the proprietary position and image of your company or product.*

   This is where your key differentiator(s) have been articulated so you stand out from the competition as an expert or have a quality or property that is unique to your company. Your audience will come to form a perception of you based on this information. For example: BMW bills itself as the ultimate driving machine.

4. *Branding helps your customer form an emotional attachment to your company.*

   Because of branding, your customer knows what to expect and what to count on from you. Branding builds trust, confidence, assurance, and a willingness to pay (more) money for your product. It supports customers' belief in you and their decision to buy your product. For example, at GE, "We bring good things to life." HBO has a clever line that explains the company by piggy-backing on its competition while implying that it is simultaneously better: "It's not TV. It's HBO."

CRITICAL TAKEAWAY: The entire purpose of branding is to create an ongoing, consistent message (in graphics and words) across all your communications. In this way, everything continuously supports and reinforces your company's goals and products.

Branding is an integral part of marketing, and therefore, it takes time. Whether you do a full-blown branding campaign or a small, targeted marketing effort, either one will require time. Just keep that in mind as you proceed.

Marketing and branding have some unexpected side effects. By branding and promoting your company and your technology/product early, you will build the morale of everyone in the company. Suddenly, all your personnel see a tangible image of what they have been working on for so long. Branding has taken the parts, made them a whole, and given them a label. This powerful validation for those within the company shows that the fruits of their labor are a viable company and commodity. This will probably be the first time they realize how important their work is to the outside world and how powerfully it will be presented. Branding and promoting your product serves as an incredible morale booster that gives employees an image to identify with.

Case History: Datalogic Research

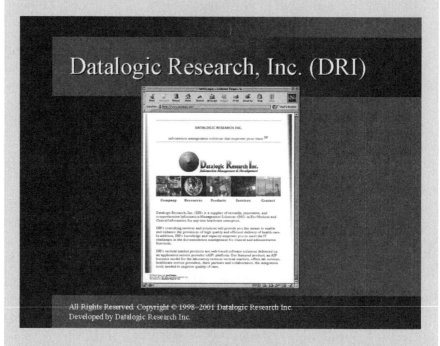

Datalogic Research, Inc. (DRI)

Here is a classic example of a company that did not start on its promotion soon enough.

Datalogic Research had developed an Application Service Provider (ASP) software model for physicians and their laboratories to use to track biopsies. They worked for at least three years on the software. As they neared the end of the software development, they were almost out of money, and they had done no promotion. They had just finished creating their web site, and only then were they willing to promote the product.

The problem was that they were behind. They had a sales cycle of at least three to six months. Because they assembled their marketing at the last moment, their survival was in doubt. The last we heard, they faced the possibility of running out of money before they made significant sales.

So, Should You Promote Your Product Before It's Ready?

Your survival may depend on your ability to generate sales interest in your product. If so, branding is an excellent way to do this. Just as sales has a cycle, branding and marketing each have a cycle, and you have seen how the two work together. This is why it is important to start building your brand and marketing it in advance of your product launch.

Lie #3

I Don't Have to Market Now Since I Have Better Science Than the Big Guys, or, My Ideas Will Be Stolen if I Market

(Some words of wisdom for the Ph.D.s, scientists and garage inventors among us.)

"A big idea (or unique science) is only as good as your ability to sell it. Many ideas have never become successful because of an inability or unwillingness to think commercially."

Scott Coleridge,
Serial CEO

We often see these attitudes in university or think tank style start-ups. That's only natural, since academia rewards ideas first. But in the business world, an idea is not a deliverable. It's a theory, an interesting direction, or an approach. And that is all it is.

You may be able to put a price tag on your idea. You may be able to get investors based on your idea. However, in today's post-bubble environment, that's much less likely to happen. The sad fact is, you cannot put your idea in a catalog or on the shelf. You cannot offer it as a service. Outside of academia, you cannot earn a living from it alone. We know. We have seen people try—and implode their start-up in the process.

Scientists are not the only ones guilty of this. The world is full of people with great ideas who cannot get out of their own way.

TRUTH #3:

If you have not addressed the commercialization aspect of your product or idea, you will have wasted a huge amount of your investor's money.

This is why the current trend with venture capitalists (VCs), angel investors, investment bankers, etc., is toward funding companies that have shown a profit. They know there is significantly less risk involved for the funders and a vista for return on their investment. They know that the ego issues that often develop in start-ups between the business guys and the scientific founder (or "big idea" guy) often hinder the commercialization process. They won't invest until these issues have been resolved.

If your product is science or technology based, you should know that many VCs and investment bankers say they will no longer touch a start-up with a scientist running the company. There are a number of good reasons for this: scientists are often too caught up in arguing about their science, they are too enamored with it, they are too arrogant/myopic to give up control to let the marketing/business experts move it into commercial viability, or all of the above. Another aspect to this is that in academia, when a discovery is announced, it's glory for the scientist alone. In business, it's glory for the company, and the scientist is only part of the team that brought the idea to market. An academically trained ego has trouble processing this. This explains an Australian VC's query when he is approached by a start-up for funding: "Have you shot the scientist yet?"

We see this in other fields as well. So, keep in mind that the world is full of wonderful ideas that fall by the wayside for these reasons.

More about Research vs. Business

Being a scientist is inherently a contradictory path to marketing a product.
Scientists are taught to develop ideas and hypotheses and to go into the lab to prove them and develop them. Scientists operate in a theoretical universe. They are not taught to think: "Well, I've got good science here, and even though I can make it better or even perfect it, I'm going to focus on turning it into a product that my company can market. Then, after we start to make money with the product, I'll go back into the lab and make the next, improved generation of the product."

Business managers, CFOs, CEOs, COOs, and sales and marketing executives think like that. This is where the internal head banging begins. If you are the scientific founder of your company and you have not brought on a business function person to complement your role and to share the power, you are in trouble. Ask any VC.

LESSON #3:
Marketing by Opening the Door and Letting Others in Who Will Help You Achieve Success

This may be difficult depending on your ability to manage the ego issues involved. And let's be clear: ego issues have sunk more ships than rocky passages. This is the same for home office entrepreneurs as it is for well-funded biotech start-ups.

One of the first hurdles is the sense of ownership and idea theft. Since scientists and inventors often come out of universities, which are notorious environments for the theft, or "sharing," of ideas, they have learned to keep a tight lid on their innovations. They know their idea is based on an insight or product modification and that makes it easy to copy. Though this lid may protect them within the scientific community, it becomes a roadblock to obtaining money. Sooner or later, you will have to market the idea, if only to raise money.

The minute you start to look for funding, you will have to share your ideas with VCs, bankers, scientists, and other investors. Even if you go to a local bank for a loan, you will have to reveal your idea, which will be in your business plan. They will all have it. Many different sets of eyes will be looking at it. That's the nature of starting a company.

Therefore, the faster you move to develop your product and get it into the world with your name on it, the more ownership you will have of it. You will make it more difficult to steal your idea, and you will start seeing revenue sooner.

Protecting Your Baby

Trademark and copyright your ideas as soon as possible. Legal arguments are often settled by ownership of the rights and the date they were filed. The decision to patent or not patent is more complex and should be discussed with your attorney.

A second hurdle is the inability to stop perfecting or working on your baby. On the one hand, perfection is often an illusion, a target just beyond where you are at the moment. On the other hand, the state of searching for perfection is a great place to hide out and a great way to avoid doing what needs to be done—which is handling all the non-inventive parts of the company. To put it another way, if Bill Gates had waited until Microsoft Word was perfected, he'd still be sitting in a garage.

A third hurdle is reluctance to allow outsiders into your company to help you bring your ideas to market by giving them the freedom they need to do the job. By freedom, we mean allowing them to determine the business focus and direction and supporting them with resources. It also means treating them as equal teammates in your business. This does not mean letting go of your baby. It means bringing in a second parent to enhance your child's growth and development.

A fourth hurdle is to stop looking for applause in all the wrong places. The business world applauds financial success and that needs to be your goal, crass as it may sound. Within this goal, you can refine your product, get recognition from your scientific and academic peers, and do what you do best. But the context shifts from academic to commercial recognition.

A fifth hurdle is being comfortable with "not knowing." Accept the fact that when it comes to marketing, you do not know how much you do not know. Here's an example: Say you've developed a better way to deliver a certain drug than the Big Pharmaceutical companies. Your product has one less side effect than theirs, but this is not an earth-shattering improvement. If it is marketed correctly, however, you could make a niche for yourself with this product improvement and build a market by taking away business from the other companies (or perhaps have your product licensed by the other companies).

Most importantly, if you build credibility through marketing yourself, it will be difficult for someone to steal your ideas and discredit your efforts. If you plan to compete against large, well-established companies in your sector, remember that for a few hundred thousand dollars (chump change for these companies), they can generate their own PR to cast doubt on the efficacy of what you are selling, researching, etc. That will have far more impact than you and your colleagues sitting around in your lab knowing that you have "better science."

A final hurdle is, no matter how good your baby is, never underestimate the big guys. Because you have not heard about it doesn't mean they aren't working on a similar idea. Even if yours is better, their ability to flood the market with product information can bury your message and your entire product/company launch.

Marketing is not always about who has the better science, products, or services, or who commercialized them first. Marketing is about creating an image and need for your product and getting people to demand it.

Case History: The Company That Could Not Become a Company

A multi-degreed scientist we know started a company with a highly regarded, well-grounded idea and science centered on one of the latest technologies. The technology was so hot that he got a lot of venture capital to develop it. Using this money, he did what he knew best: He hired more Ph.D.s from the university that sponsored him and used them to forward the progress of the licensed technology. Ultimately, what he did was create a university department in private industry with himself as chairman. It's like mixing metaphors, or in this case, business models. You cannot do it and succeed.

He thought he was a fabulous success, and indeed, a lot of interest was generated in the science. However, after five years, all he had done was raise millions of dollars. He never hired a businessman and never attempted to commercialize the technology. In short, he built himself his own ivory tower, and it crumbled because all of his investors wanted to see a return on their investments. The company's board of directors, who were part of the university that helped develop the technology, wanted to see it commercialized as well. Had this happened, everyone would have been rewarded for their contribution.

The university would have earned licensing fees and become more world renowned for its wonderful, edgy science. It would have attracted more funding and more talented students who wanted to study there. The investors would have made a return on their investment. The scientific founder would have become rich and famous and would have been freed to move to bigger, better projects with an enhanced reputation for his ability to deliver a marketable product, which would have generated more funding.

Instead, the scientist lost his job and disappeared into oblivion. Last we heard, the company was crippled and desperately seeking more money to turn itself around with a business leader at the helm. It may have been too late.

So, Do You Have to Market Now Even If You Have a Better Idea than the Other Companies?

Yes, you do. No matter how good your idea. Your investors will insist on it, and your creation deserves it. As an inventor, you know you have to toot your own horn to get grants, get published, and get ahead. Marketing is tooting your own horn to move forward in a new and different arena.

Lie #4

I Have to Show a Profit Before I Can Market

"Branding is a powerful marketing tool for selling products. And if you don't believe it, try naming a company that manufactures light bulbs other than GE! Start-ups should start immediately."

Denise Drace-Brownell,
Managing Director and Senior Counsel, DDB, Associates, LLC

In the best possible world, life would work like that. But think about it logically. Where is that profit going to come from? Don't you need to find those customers? How will you do that?

Do you have customers lined up? Are you a spin-off company expecting your mother company to buy and/or market your product, service, or science? Have you built your business with a second mortgage on your home so you're committed to your product's development and feel all the money should go there first?

Perhaps you feel that putting money into marketing is adding to your exposure and you are extended as far as you want to go.

Is marketing something you still feel hazy about? It's understandable that you might want to avoid putting money into an effort about which you don't have 100 percent understanding.

Is it possible that your time and energy are stretched to the max, so marketing has to wait? Waiting until you have a profit seems like a good rationalization, but it's really a cop-out. Finally, what's your definition of profit? You may have a big investment in this product. Do you have to pay that off before you feel you are making a profit?

TRUTH #4:

You will never make a profit if you do not drive customers to your product and give them a reason to buy it.

People cannot buy your product if they do not know where it is or if it even exists. Getting the word out is how you generate sales and bring in profits.

Here's another way to look at this. Separate building the product from building the company. They are different. Research and development is how you create the product. Marketing is how you create the company. They are inter-dependent, but if you have a strong product and a weak company, your product may never get the recognition it deserves. Yet a strong company with a weak product can succeed.

Suppose you have a drug that has failed FDA trials, or you have a product held up in manufacturing, or your product has failed for some other reason. A company whose management team has a strong marketing sense can still sell what it excels at and keep the company going as it improves the product. The management team can move to something else or switch the company's direction altogether. Because the company has an understanding of marketing, it does not have to throw in the towel if something goes wrong.

For instance, the company can contract itself out as a research service with specific expertise (often the same expertise used to develop the product), or it can market its consultancy skills, technology, or a related functional product.

Marketing builds a plan of action so, no matter what happens, the company always knows its direction. Marketing supports the company in being nimble and responsive enough to change in the marketplace.

What does this have to do with making a profit before you market?

A company with a marketing plan will be building the company's image as you build the company's product or service, which is true no matter how large or small the company. This means you must build marketing into your fundraising efforts. All funders, including VCs, banks, and angels, recognize the need to get the word out about the product.

In financially sensitive times, this may seem imprudent. In fact, a business plan that does not show an understanding of the need to prepare the market for your product will present your company as being naïve or inexperienced and may remove you from the funding arena.

VC and funding institutions want to see management that understands the entire picture of starting a company. Accommodating this need for marketing in your business plan is one way to show you are preparing your company for success and prof-itability.

Marketing does not have to be a big-ticket item but does have to be well thought out so you allocate your money wisely and get the most bang for your buck. Yes, you must put some time against it no matter how stretched you are feeling. We guarantee that a lit-tle quality time early on will save time and money in the long run.

For instance, during the great dot-com boom, starts-ups had huge amounts of money for marketing, much of which was spent willy-nilly, without a true plan or understanding of the return on investment that spending so much should have produced. Remember those multimillion-dollar commercials that ran during the Super Bowl? That's a fine place to be if you're Budweiser or IBM and have already created massive brand recognition for yourself. It's not a good place for a start-up with no national recognition.

Other monies were spent on billboards and transit ads where the messages were so obscure, nobody knew what the company did, what the benefit was, who the audience was, or why the prod-uct even existed. At one point, almost every ad in major news magazines was a technology ad, but few were speaking to the cor-rect audience. Most of these were vanity ads from companies with too much money and bad advice. Obviously, we're not suggesting your company take this route.

A more appropriate plan would be a direct mail campaign—post-cards or letters—directing people to a well-constructed web site or to a knowledgeable company salesperson. This will build the com-pany in a fiscally sensible way by building its image though expo-sure to the proper audience. Since the goal is to have people ask for the product as it is launched, you could simultaneously inte-grate a PR effort. Have "experts" in the company available at trade shows, on trade show panels, quoted in trade magazines, and writing articles. This becomes ammunition to put on your web site as proof of your company's expertise.

If you want to educate people and you have a larger budget (but less than for a Super Bowl ad), you may choose to do something to attract attention, a programmed learning sweepstakes, for instance. In this promotional effort, you offer a prize of significant value to people who visit your web site and are able to answer questions about your product or company. The information/answers can only be found by reading the content of the web site. In short, you are driving a targeted audience to your web site and compelling them to read specific information about your company and its products.

In this way, you force their exposure to information that helps to build your brand and sell your products.

Simple tactics like these help you prepare the market for your product and support it in generating revenue from the beginning. This is what we call branding. If you wait to initiate this kind of process, you will find yourself doing it as your full-fledged product or service sits on the shelf losing money. If your product has a long sales cycle, you will be waiting longer.

Put another way, you are building your company's brand and developing the foundations for customer loyalty. This will enhance the product's perceived value and allow you to charge accordingly.

LESSON #4:

Generating Profit by Maximizing Your Product's Perceived Value

What happens when companies invest in building their company? Here are three examples in the consumer products world.

1. We have heard that GE attributes incremental sales of $10 billion each year to the power of its brand name. When generic soft white light bulbs, for instance, are sold next to the GE brand, nine out of ten people buy the GE product and fork over 25 percent more even though the products have the same performance specs on the package. For all we know, GE could be producing the generic bulb as well.

2. We've been told that when consumers were asked to rate a floor tile, they gave it a 50 percent favorable rating. When they were told it was an Armstrong floor tile, the approval rating jumped to 80 percent for the same tile.

3. In a classic marketing taste test done in Texas, people were given an unmarked container of ice cream and then compared it with one marked with a well-known local brand. They preferred the one with the brand name even though both were the same.

Now, transfer this example to your business arena and see where it is operating in your particular niche. Work your way through lab equipment, hardware products, services, or retailers. Are there brands that you or your people prefer? If you are a scientist, do you have a molecular preparation you feel is better because it comes from a certain company? A particular type of test tube? Measuring device? Mixing device? You get the point. Even if every product in a given category is at parity, chances are you or your colleagues will prefer one brand because of your perception of its value.

CRITICAL TAKEAWAY: When preparing to market a product, pay attention to the branding phenomenon. Failure to do so is the reason why many new products, superior to existing products, do not get the attention and sales they deserve.

By investing in building your company's name, you are creating value that will pay off on a continuing basis. In the course of building the brand, you are instilling customer trust and confidence. This leads to loyalty and a higher perceived value of service. This, in turn, will support better pricing and lead to higher profits, as shown in the illustration below.

WHAT IS THE VALUE OF A BRAND?

5
Higher
Profits

4
Higher Revenues

3
Higher Perceived
Value of Service

2
Customer Loyalty

1
Customer Trust and Confidence

Case History: Avalon Chrystie Place and Whole Foods Market

Avalon Chrystie Place is a new luxury rental building being constructed on New York City's Lower East Side. During the early phases of the construction process, the building, which runs the length of a whole city block, was surrounded by scaffolding with posters on it. The posters announced the building's construction, directed passers-by to the web site and phone number, and described the building as a rental. (In New York City, new rental units are a big deal.)

The posters announced the attractive amenities the building was going to offer. One amenity was featured on its own poster, which announced that Whole Foods Market would come to the building soon.

All this information created a buzz almost a year prior to the building's opening and well in advance of Whole Foods' arrival. Whole Foods was used as a selling point for the residence, since a supermarket in an apartment building is an amenity. The announcement let the neighborhood residents and workers know about, anticipate, and plan for shopping in a well-branded supermarket at a new venue.

After the construction scaffolding came down, new posters appeared in the windows of the building repeating the same exciting news. Posters, web sites, and related marketing materials cost money to create far in advance of a single dime coming in as revenue for either of the new venues. By spending this money in advance, the rental building and the supermarket improved their chances of being filled and supported on the day they opened.

So, Do You Have to Make A Profit Before You Can Market?

Wait that long and you might not have a company. It sounds drastic, but it can be uncomfortably close to the truth. The marketplace is full of good ideas and great products. The difference between the ones that are and are not successful is usually marketing and not quality.

Lie #5

I Only Need a Web Site

"Today's business owner is surrounded by countless competitors out to get their customers and their business. The array of weapons used by these competitors is both extensive and sophisticated. To settle on a one-step defense of developing only a web site is to risk losing the war."

Louis Gaburo,
*Acting Director of the Enterprise Development Center
at New Jersey Institute of Technology*

You only need a web site. Well, yes and no. That statement is full of assumptions. Let's look at some of our favorites that we hear all the time:

"Web sites are easy to put up. Anyone can do it."

When it comes to web sites, everybody is an expert, and they are all free with their opinions. Yes, you can have a high-school kid or your in-house tech guy put up your web site. You can also do it yourself. After all, who's going to know the difference? But, have you ever really examined one of those web sites?

Web sites put up by people inexperienced in marketing strategy are often naïve and poorly conceived in terms of communication, information presentation, navigation, messages, branding, etc. In short, they seem unprofessional in their look, content, organization, or messaging.

Do yourself a favor. Go on the Web, check out some of these web sites, and ask yourself these questions:

- Does the home page have something that immediately appeals to you to make you want to stay on the web site?
- Does the web site make it easy for you to access the information you need?
- Is the web site visually and graphically appealing?

- Does the web site properly reflect the quality of the company?
- Does the web site make you feel the company is trustworthy, professional, and reliable?
- Does the web site make you want to purchase the company's product or services?

Get the idea? There is more to a web site than HTML formatting with an "open for business" sign on the home page.

"We do not need a marketing budget. We just need a web site budget."

What are you going to put on the web site? Your company's name? Your company's logo? Do you have a name or a logo? Are they trademarked? Do you have a basic marketing message (your "elevator pitch"), a benefit line, or a succinct description of the company, such as boilerplate copy (a paragraph that describes your company and is used consistently at the end of every press release)?

Your web site should reflect these marketing basics, starting at the home page. Do you know what kind of information your visitors are looking for? Remember, this is the Web. You have about three seconds to get their attention before they bounce back to the search engine.

You need to determine all these factors before work starts on your web site. Therefore, you do need a marketing budget. Or you need to split your web site budget and put some of it toward defining your marketing basics and objectives. Handle these issues and you can put up a less expensive web site that works harder for you.

"Content is no big deal. We already have a business plan and product descriptions. We can use those."

A web site is a dynamic interactive medium, and you need to put up information your customers want to see. If you do not, you may lose them. Your business plan has probably done a good job in getting funding, which is one purpose of a business plan. However, a business plan is not a marketing document. Information will need to be retooled as selling points. Writing for the Web is different than writing for paper or a brochure. Web writing needs to be quick and to the point. Offer top-line information and drill-downs with detailed information for those who want it. As important as the content is on a web site, the organization of the content is equally important.

How many times have you landed on a home page that does not tell you what the company does or if this is the kind of company you sought? Worse, how many times have you wound up on a web site that takes you on a drilling expedition to search for information? How much of that will you do before you leave? And how often have you landed on a home page that is so busy and disorganized that it's a struggle to find the information you want even though you're sure it's there, somewhere?

The information in your business plan and product description(s) is information you need and think is important. But what do your customers want to read? Chances are it's not something they want to chew through. (Let's face it: How many people have mission statements that really light your fire?) So, a business plan is a good starting point from which to develop web content, but it is only a starting point.

"We'll just do a placeholder site for now and come back and do something fancier later."

Will your audience come back later? Placeholders can work. They do give you a presence on the Web. They offer basic information, e.g., whom to contact, location. They can buy you some time but not much. Too often, people get caught up in their product development and forget about their web site. Consequently, their placeholder site does not reflect the sophistication of their company, products, and services.

So, by all means, put up a placeholder site, but do not let it become a substitute for a well-designed web site. This web site is the front door to your company. Do not leave it unpainted and unfinished for too long, or no one will want to visit or believe your company is serious about doing business. They may assume that your products are as unfinished as your web image. Perception is everything.

"The competition's web site looks simple. We can do that."

Can you? Are you sure their web site is simple? Take a look at the navigation. Does it easily get you to the information you want? Does it have all the links you need to move through the web site quickly? Are the menus extensive enough and obvious enough to help you drill down to what you want? Is the information presented in a way that seems intuitive, a way that makes sense to you? Is the text succinct and on point? Do you come away with a good sense of the company and of the value of their products and services? Are you finding the information you need?

It takes a lot of background work and thinking to make a complex web site look simple. For instance, take a look at the Terminix web site at www.terminix.com.

Getting rid of bugs is not a pretty subject. But this web site has a classy fashion feel. It communicates a sense of home comfort and security from the start, which makes you feel good about exploring the company's services. The web site predisposes you to contact the company. Information about specific pests and problems is easy to locate, informative, and interestingly displayed. In fact, wandering around the web site is fun despite the wide array of information and drill-downs.

"The competition's web site is sophisticated. We need to be like that, too."

Do you? This is the age-old problem of keeping up with the Joneses. The best way not to stand out is to copy everybody else. Your company, your science, your product and your management are unique. Your web site should reflect you and should not sell your competition. If their web site is out there first and you look like them, you run the risk of blending in with their message or looking like a me-too product.

Here's an example of a company that had the Joneses keeping up with them: A pharmaceutical company introduced a skin medicine. It was the third medication in the category to hit the marketplace. The product had benefits that surpassed the two competitors but had to overcome being the last one to market. The company put up a web site that was not particularly expensive, but was researched and designed better and spoke directly to the end users (in this case, patients) in their own language. The web site, and the sales it generated, blew the other two competitors out of the water. This web site was so successful that the two competitor companies copied elements and promotions from it in their next web site upgrades. This reflects poorly on the copycat brand managers, ad agencies, and web developers because they abandoned their own branding to imitate their competitor, which could boomerang. By copying the successful web site's branding elements, they were promoting the other product.

"We have a substantial budget and want a web site with all the bells and whistles. Our science is flashy and high-end, and our web site should reflect that."

Just because you have the money and the technical expertise to do something doesn't necessarily mean you should. Technology should serve your message. For instance, some people love Flash animation on a web site so much, they want their whole web site created in Flash. Flash web sites are more difficult to change because of the nature of the programming. This becomes a particular obstacle if your copy has been programmed in Flash. Every copy change requires reprogramming, which can be expensive and time-consuming. Also, because you love the animation on other web sites does not mean it will work or be pertinent to your web site. Animation should serve your message.

The point is to put the technology to work for you in a strategically savvy way.

Keep two other things in mind. First, not everyone has high-speed Internet access and can download all the bells and whistles easily. (We know some venture capitalists, or VCs, who made clients take the Flash off their web site. They could not download the web site because they still had dial-up accounts.) Second, if a web site looks overproduced, people (including your investors) may think you are wasting money and are not a fiscally responsible company. They may also think your efforts are not focused on product development but on Web technology. You might even look like a (gasp!) dot-com. This is a terrible image for a start-up.

Before the dot-com bomb, and the recent nuclear winter in investing, some VCs were known to check out the parking lot of West Coast start-ups to see what kind of cars the employees drove. A lot filled with pricey cars meant the start-up was not handling its finances properly. An over-produced web site could be a similar signal.

"In my business, the only thing people look at is a web site, so why do anything else?"

We agree that a web site is critical, particularly in a technology or retail field. In today's world, a business without a web site almost ceases to exist. However, if you think that limiting your marketing to a web site will save you time and money, forget about it. All you will be limiting is your company's potential.

A web site is only one tactical element in a successful marketing plan. It may be the biggest and most important, but it remains a part of an overall effort. That effort begins with the development of your logo, your tag line, your copy, and other branding elements. In other words, you need to have your basic branding finished and displayed on your web site to reflect the who and what of your company.

This is particularly true in technologies, such as biotechnology, information technology, nanotechnology, and chemical technologies. Your web site is the front door to your business, but it is not the only door. Ask yourself what are you going to hand out at trade shows. Will you have a trade show booth? What will your materials look like? How will you drive visitors to your web site? Even an accountant, lawyer, chiropractor, jewelry store—virtually everyone in business—needs some kind of handout to take advantage of trade shows, meetings, and other opportunities. These are all doorways to your business.

There are a number of different ways to drive people to your web site, and we will discuss them later in this chapter. How to drive people is a critical consideration in making your web site successful.

"We have a small budget and think a web site is plenty to achieve our purposes."

If you have a small budget, you must have your branding elements in place. In the long run, it will save you time and money. We strongly suggest you have a logo you like, a phrase that explains your company's benefit, and a graphic "look" that can be applied to your web site and to other materials later.

"Our colleagues said not to pay too much for a web site. They only paid $3,500 [or $10,000 or $25,000] for theirs."

Start by comparing apples to apples. With web sites, that comparison is difficult to make because so much of what goes into a site is invisible.

Check out the web sites of the people who are telling you not to pay too much. Ask them how many hits they are getting. Ask how many of those hits are being converted into phone calls, sales, or repeat business.

When you get to the web sites, look at them with a disinterested eye and see if you are getting all the information you need quickly or if the sites are navigation nightmares. Spend some time on a search engine and look for these web sites. When you use key words, do the sites show up? Then look for the competitors' sites and visit those. How do they stack up against your friends' web sites? Finally, ask yourself this: Does the look and language of the web site lend itself to other materials, such as brochures and trade booths? Or will you have to start from scratch when you develop other materials?

A few thousand dollars is not going to deliver your branding, a web strategy, and an understanding of your customers and what they need to see on your web site. Nor will it cover design, copy-writing, and information architecture. If people tell you it will cost only a couple of thousand dollars to achieve all of that, make them prove it.

A successful web site requires time, effort, and money, but by planning it wisely, you can keep costs down.

"Our information is dense; we need a lot of pages and layers."

As the Internet has matured, research has shown that the average visitor to a site gives it approximately 3 seconds to deliver a reason to stay. And people have only one reason to stay: finding what they came for immediately.

For this reason, the trend over the last couple of years has been to provide much of the meaty information within one drill-down from the home page. This often means multiple menus on the home page. These menus need to organize and present information attractively and efficiently. Drop-down menus, mouse-overs, pop-ups, and other techniques can be used to keep the home page clean and attractive. The organization of the information is called information architecture. This includes what information is presented, how it is presented at every level, and how it is connected to other information on every level of the web site.

"As soon as I can get an estimate for a web site that I like, I will figure out what to put on it."

You can start this way, but you will be at the mercy of the web designers, who will probably give you an estimate based on a web site with the usual sections: Who we are, What we do, Press releases, and Contact us. Avoid this approach. You will not be happy with an off-the-shelf solution. You want a web site customized to your needs.

We know you are busy with your new business, but you need to invest some time up front to determine what you want on your site. Here is the information you need to consider and questions you need to ask to direct the web developer in producing the result you want.

- How many "pages" (screens) are you going to need on your site?

- Will you present your information on long, scrolling pages, or on separate pages?

- Do you need/want animation or Flash?
- Do you need/want sound and/or music?
- Will you supply the graphics and photography, or must new art and photography be created?
- Will you need/want streaming video?
- Do you need an interactive database?
- Will the site need secure password-protected areas?
- Will you be selling a product? Will you need transactional capabilities?
- Will you need a search function?
- Will you need the ability to enlarge the site down the road?

Here are three basic ways to start organizing your web site thinking.

1. The easiest way is to outline the site as you would outline a report or article. This format lets you plot out your site anywhere, including on a plane or at a bar on the proverbial napkin. Though this gets you started, it does not give you a big picture of how the different parts of the web site will relate to each other.

2. Diagramming a site gives you many more insights.

   Here's a chart diagram that can be done by hand or in an Excel spread sheet. It shows each level (hierarchy) of a site for a manufacturing company and how each drill-down works.

Level 1	Level 2	Level 3	Level 4	Level 5	Notes
Home page					
	About Us				Shows photo of building. Overview
		Management Team			Names and titles, quick bios, group shot
		Board of Directors			Names, titles, quick bios (write), head shots
		Company History			Discusses recent merger, new goals
	Interior Products				
		Product Catalog			Use revised product sheets?
			Enlarged view of each product (30 pages)		

continued on next page

Level 1	Level 2	Level 3	Level 4	Level 5	Notes
				Link to video of valves	Get video from Sales
	Exterior Products				
		Product Catalog			
			Enlarged view of each product (20 pages)		
	Repair Shops				
		Addresses & Phone Info			
			Directions: Link to Mapquest		
	Contact Us				
		List Info			Include sales reps info

Level 1 is your home page. Level 2 lists all sections that will have a link (button) on the home page. If each of those sections links to additional information, list those links on Level 2, and so on. As you lay out your approach, make notes to yourself in the far right column. This puts all your thoughts on paper in a manner you can share with coworkers or web developers.

Charting helps you determine the information's hierarchy and forces you to look at how information can be put into "buckets" to make it more manageable. The goal is to make it easy for visitors to your site to find the information they want without having to wade through what they don't want.

3. A more efficient way to map out a site is to use a chart that resembles an organizational chart. This one happens to be on its side. Here again, the information is in levels, and this chart allows you to show more sophisticated linkages. The square boxes show static pages that do not change, and the multiple box squares represent multiple pages of similar content. The rounded box shows pages with dynamic content that can be changed. In this case, the dynamic page is a schedule to be updated regularly by someone in the company using a template.

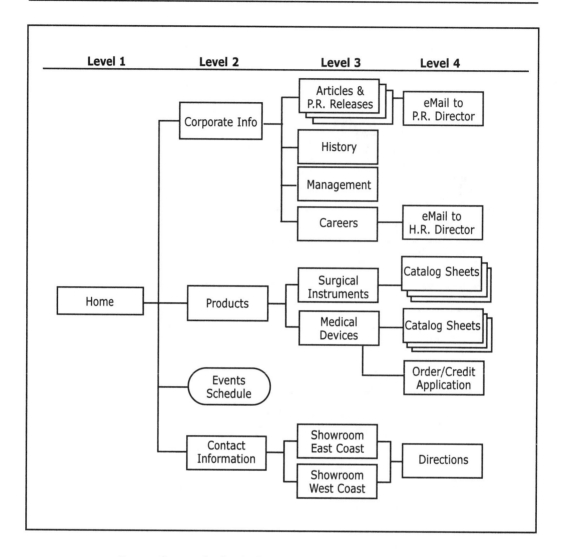

Regardless of which format you use to map out your web site, you must think it through before you go to your web developer. If you show the web developer what you have in mind, you will get better feedback and will save time. Plus, your developer will be able to give you a realistic estimate for building the site.

"We have a brochure. We'll just put that on the web."

Web sites come in two categories. A brochure web site is a static version of a brochure translated to the Web. A new-generation web site more fully utilizes the medium's ability to organize and deliver multifaceted information in accessible, intuitive, and interactive ways.

Brochure Type

MFX's elegant brochure site (www.mfxfairfax.com) mirrors this start-up's print materials. The web site's graphics, as well as its tone and manner, reflect the company's branding. The company's tagline (Moving at the speed of opportunity), logo, and industry focus are clearly stated on the home page. Information is organized traditionally behind five buttons (Company Overview, Products & Services, News & Events, Careers at MFX, and Contact MFX). Below each button is a visual icon and a top line of information that answers immediate questions a visitor might have (Who is MFX? What can we do for you?). Within each section, you have additional menus for drill-downs and contact information for the sales rep for that product or service.

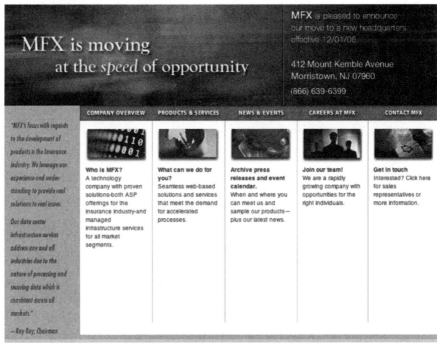

Products & Services

COMPANY OVERVIEW   PRODUCTS & SERVICES   NEWS & EVENTS   CAREERS AT MFX   CONTACT MFX

Over 70% of all large enterprise software projects fail... more often than not because of a lack of true understanding about the business practices being automated.

MFX Products and Services

Welcome to the new reality — Internet-based products and services that turn costly, paper-based business processes into a fast, effortless flow of information.

Importantly, these are products designed by insurance professionals for use by insurance professionals.

These solutions and services simplify the multi-layered processes surrounding the sale and processing of insurance products. They offer seamless, well tested, intuitive solutions designed to meet today's demand for accelerated processes...faster and more economically than developing them yourself.

SecureSource
MFX infrastructure outsourcing services allow clients to be free from the time consuming and costly task of managing their infrastructure.

ClaimsAssure
A highly intuitive processing system able to assemble, display and help adjudicate claims quickly.

RiskVault
A streamlined web-based environment that speeds claims handling while significantly reducing costs.

GlobalAssist
Outsourcing services that deliver IT expertise plus industry know-how and a better return on your dollars.

ServiceAssist
Services to assist in designing, developing and implementing infrastructure solutions to meet a company's

WriteNow
An eCommerce platform that simplifies and accelerates sales of rules-based insurance products.

ProcessSure
BPO services where insurers can streamline their back office processes, reduce costs, manage compliance issues more efficiently and free themselves to focus on revenue generation.

CorporateShield
Today's IT managers need flexible security roadmaps that adjust rapidly to ongoing and emerging threats. Our multi-disciplinary teams help clients effectively identify, assess, implement and manage security and privacy solutions.

ManagedSolutions
Accelerate your IT environment with a knowledgeable partner who can deliver the economy you seek.

VitalImages

New-Generation Type

Liberty Science Center's web site (www.lsc.org) takes full advantage of the Web's flexibility to deliver immediate access to a great deal of information all within one click. While the home page graphically offers you six distinct sections with 10+ buttons, the interior pages have mouse-over menus that give you approximately 53 options. All the drill-down options are pertinent to their subsection. This architecture allows you to navigate a large amount of information intuitively depending on where your mindset takes you.

New-generation sites like this allow you to access most of the information with only one click, thus avoiding the frustration of hunting and clicking your way through the site.

NOTE: Because the Web is a dynamic medium, these web site examples may have changed since publication of this book.

Both types of web sites can organize information in a way that communicates easily and quickly. Lifting your brochure and adapting it for the Web can save time and money since much of the work has been done. However, starting from scratch and developing a new-generation site can add an experiential element to the web site that brings people back and enhances its relevancy.

"I have a brochure, so I do not need a web site. [Or] I have a web site, so I do not need a brochure."

The fact is, one does not replace the other. You cannot hand out a web site at a trade show or mail it to a hot prospect. On the other hand, a web site gives potential clients, investors, media, and prospects immediate access to your information. You can control who sees your brochure. You cannot control who goes to your web site or what they will look at once they get there.

With a brochure, you can also control the order in which the information is presented and lay out the story linearly. A web site is a non-linear presentation of information that allows people to jump into and visit pages according to their whim. In fact, a search engine may take a visitor directly to an inside page rather than the home page.

On the other hand, you can easily update a web site and it can hold more information, important considerations for an evolving company. Updating a brochure takes longer and is more costly even if you are only updating an insert sheet.

The bottom line: You probably need a web site and a brochure. The order in which you create them depends on your needs.

"Getting people to the site will be easy because the search engines will do that."

A search engine will help people find you, but it's not quite as simple as you might think. You must ensure the search engines will find your web site when someone searches with a relevant word. More importantly, you want the search engines to list your web site on the first two or three pages. So, it helps to know some basics about how the engines work.

More and more, search engines make use of robots, also called spiders, bots, or crawlers. These tiny applications travel actual links between pages as well as the links people make going from web site to web site as they search. When the crawlers hit a new web site, they send the information back to the search engine's database, where it is indexed according to subject matter.

Once, search engines relied on keywords to determine the relevancy of a web site's subject matter. These were found in the web site's content and were included in the web site's programming, but programmers learned how to "stuff" a site with keywords, fooling the engines into listing the web site higher up on the searcher's results page.

Search engines have overcome this trickery by looking for relevancy among the linkages. If visitors to your site visit other sites with the same subject matter, it creates relevancy and helps place your site higher in the listing. The more a web site gets this kind of traffic, the more relevant it will become to the search engine. Keywords placed in the meta-tags, headlines, subheads, and first paragraph of the web page help. Use them sparingly because some engines will penalize a site that jams too many into its design.

You can register your web site yourself with some of the major search engines. Google and MSN Search make this process easy and free. Go to the web sites and look for the "Submit Your Site" link (note that you may really have to dig to find these options). Yahoo has free registration, but you first have to provide personal information to submit your site. Other engines may charge a fee. Almost all of them offer paid "ads" or sponsor links that can steer surfers to your company. Touring the search engine sites will give you an idea of what opportunities exist in this area.

Search Engine Optimization (SEO) can also help you land higher up in the listings.

Many companies specialize in SEO. Some submit your Uniform Resource Locator (URL) to all the search engines. Other companies will help you structure your site and content to be more attractive to the search engines. You can find these companies on the Web, using a search engine, naturally. Unfortunately, SEO has gotten a bad rap because of poor and even illicit company practices. Getting recommendations from happy customers is the best way to find a good SEO. Google's web site, in its Webmaster Help Center section, offers good advice about using

Print Vs. Interactive

These different terms explain why the presentation of information is different on a web site than it is in a brochure. Web sites that are direct lifts of a brochure can work well as a starting point, but by the time you do your second-generation web site, you should be taking fuller advantage of the Web.

A new-generation web site can hold considerably more information than a brochure without being too dense or overwhelming. By taking the time to research what your visitors want to know immediately, you can put that information in their face first and, simultaneously, give them the opportunity to drill down for more information.

SEO companies. MSN Search offers guidelines on how to have your programmer prepare your site for successful indexing (again, you will have to drill down for this information).

CRITICAL TAKEAWAY: Every web site is a marketing site. Some sell. Some do nothing. Some un-sell.

TRUTH #5:

A web site is a good place to start, but it cannot produce results if it lives in a vacuum.

It's one thing to be listed on search engines. But that alone will not generate enough traffic and doesn't answer the underlying question: How will you drive people to your web site?

One vehicle is direct mail such as postcards, letters, and mailers. Another is ads in trade journals and newspapers. (Do not underestimate the importance of your help wanted ads, because job applicants on all levels will research you through your web site.) Still another is press releases and other public relations events.

To do any of these, you will need your basics in hand. You will need a logo, a commanding claim or tag line, and key messaging about your company that can be slapped onto a postcard or any of the vehicles above and sent out.

Your web site will need product and technology marketing descriptions. These should be consistent with other materials, so when prospects arrive at your web site, they have a sense of recognition and relationship. The reverse also holds true. After visiting your web site, a prospect who sees your ad, your business card, or your brochure and convention panels at a trade show should have a sense of recognition and relationship. In other words, your web site is constantly enhancing and reaffirming your company's image in the marketplace and vice versa.

To use a popular aphorism, you never have enough money/time to do it right, but you always have enough money/time to do it over. Because of this, think through your branding and get it right from the start.

LESSON #5:

Knowing the Basics About a Web Site Before You Start One

One of the best ways to put up a good web site is to know key web site facts before you initiate your web site project. The following

Ten Commandments should help you put up an effective web site the first time.

I. Use Professional Services

- Check the developers' references. Ask what the developers are like to work with. Are they responsive? Do they listen? Do they understand marketing goals and needs? Do they meet deadlines? Is their technology flawless? Do they beta test thoroughly so their sites work easily and properly on all platforms (for example, on both Macs and PCs)?
- Look at other sites the developers have built. Are you comfortable with the look, feel, and usage? Are the web sites appropriate to the kind of businesses they represent?
- Make sure hosting companies are reliable and will exist for a long time. If possible, speak to others who are hosting with them.
- Ensure your host service is accessible 24/7 by phone as well as e-mail. Ensure good customer service.

II. Know Your Users

- Research them and know what they want.
- In what order do they want information? What's most important to them (not you)? Give it to them their way.
- Know how to talk to each user who will be visiting your web site and organize it accordingly.
- Speak to your users in their own language. Teenagers, physicians, auto mechanics, and stay-at-home moms have different voices.

III. Know What Results You Want from Your Web Site

- Identify what success means to you.
- Know how you will measure success/results before you start building the web site. What do you want the web site to generate? Sales? Investors? Phone calls?
- Regularly review what success means to you and make necessary adjustments.

IV. Reflect Your Message Branding

- Make sure the logo, tag line, and key messaging are present.
- Make sure the web site's messaging is consistent with other company communications.

V. Make Your Navigation and Architecture Intuitive

- Place all core information no more than one click from the home page.
- Use user research to guide the organization of and access to the content.
- Make sure downloads are quick and smooth.
- Make sure the web site is accessible to high-end and low-end computer users.
- Test your web site so it works on all types of computers and browsers.

VI. Communicate Clearly

- Do not assume all your visitors will be familiar with your product or its terms. Do not talk down to your users and do not talk over their heads.
- Keep content short, concise, and to the point.
- Communicate in ways that speed understanding, such as with charts, examples, and case studies.

VII. Drive Users to Your Site

- Get on search engines.
- Optimize your web site's ability to attract the search engines.
- Use direct mail, direct marketing, and advertising to generate traffic.
- List the web site on all your communications materials.
- Search out listing possibilities on industry-specific web sites.
- Research pay-per-click to see if it is appropriate for your business.

VIII. Use the Site to Begin a Relationship with Your Customers

- Offer information or incentives that cannot be found anywhere else.
- Give customers every opportunity to interact and get involved with you, such as with e-mail, bulletin boards, speaking engagement notices, and trade shows you will be attending.
- Make sure your web site tells people how to contact you. Include directions, phone numbers, and geographical location.

IX. Maintain Your Web Site

- Give this responsibility to only one person, preferably a technical/graphics individual who reports to senior management.
- Make sure that person gets all the latest information that needs to be posted on the web site in a timely fashion and knows the vendors, passwords, etc.
- Ask for all original graphic files and HTML files (including Photoshop files, Illustrator files, jpegs, and gifs) from professional service firms so your company owns all original content.
- Make sure all information concerning the hosting company, including contacts, e-mails, and passwords, is written down and kept in several places within your company.

X. Move at Web Speed

- Put up your web site as soon as you can.
- Generate traffic as quickly as possible.
- Update the web site regularly.

As you can see, a web site is a living, breathing entity that represents your company globally, 24/7. It requires care and nourishment and cannot be allowed to languish, go out of date, or become tired-looking.

We almost hate to bring this up, but it's often forgotten: If you move or change your phone number, change the web site information as well.

Case History: Xenopharm

This company had nearly completed its branding project and had almost finalized its tag line and logo design when it initiated its web site. It knew that these elements were prerequisites to building an effective web site and a successful brand.

This company is unusual because the CEO had significant marketing background in addition to having previously started another company. He therefore understood all the "minimum" elements he needed for "only a web site." He had the logo, his commanding claim and company description, a mission statement, and enough information to have meat on the web site.

The CEO's priority in establishing the site was recruitment. The company needed to recruit Ph.D.s to further develop their proprietary science prior to initiating the next round of financing. Messaging was developed that became the basis of claims. Emphasis was placed on the copy in the section of the web site that focused on what it was like to work in the company and the lure and advantages for a Ph.D. to live and work in southern California. The secondary focus was on the proprietary science, which would appeal to the target group. People were driven to the web site through traditional classified ads in the appropriate technical journals.

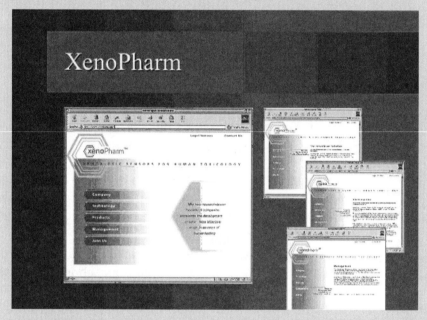

Strategically, this web site was intended strictly as a recruitment tool with a life span of approximately six months. Once it achieved its purpose, it would be removed, and a new, more elaborate site would be uploaded to the same URL.

Case History: GeneWiz

This biotechnology company does custom research and sells all forms of DNA, gene sequencing, testing, and cloning kits. These are relatively inexpensive items with a short sales cycle. GeneWiz began with a primitive web site that had all the basic information but looked amateurish and unprofessional. Ordering was handled by having the customer fill out a downloadable Adobe Acrobat file and fax, snail mail, or phone in the order.

To expand their services and grow beyond their small clientele, the company realized it needed to put up a more sophisticated and professional web site. This would allow it to communicate expanded services to existing clients and a full range of services to new clients and to project an image of trust and reliability to all of its audiences. Here is the home page of the new site:

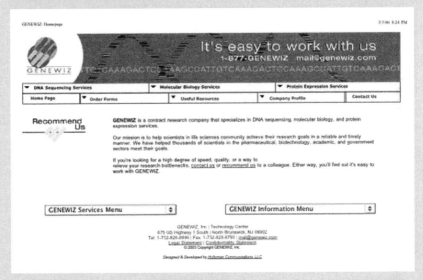

In addition to revised graphics and improved navigation, the new site featured enhancements, such as drop-down menus that organized and categorized services and information and provided instant one-click access. A menu bar across the top handled the standard information like contact, company profile, order forms, and the company's three most popular services. Additionally, ordering was simplified by programming in a transactional capability so clients could order online.

On the first web site, the tag line/claim was "Bringing expert services to biomedical research communities." If you are in the biomedical community this is a given, so the tag line conveyed no new information. The new tag line, "It's easy to work with us," expressed a true benefit based on customer feedback. This important selling point set up an expectation of good service fast, which was the key differentiator of GeneWiz. To see this site live go to www.holtzmancom.com/genewiz.

So, Is a Web Site All You Need? Probably Not If You Really Want to Produce Results.

Assuming you have registered your web site with the search engines and that your key words, meta tags, etc., are apt, you will get some traffic. But do not rely on the kindness of strangers to build your business. The more visitors you drive to the site, the more success you will have in building your company's presence in your marketplace. The more strategic your web site's message, the more likely you are to convert these new relationships into customers.

Lie #6

I Need to Do Public Relations First

"Public relations, especially media relations, allow start-ups to generate awareness the most cost-effectively. Relationships make things happen, so think of building relationships with your key publics as a critical part of your business."

Christine Terashita,
Marketing Consultant

Your reasoning probably goes like this: "PR is an inexpensive way to build market, so let's start there." You're right—PR can be a cost-effective way to build market and brand recognition. It can also be a total waste of time.

If you think PR is just a matter of writing a press release announcing something that has happened in your company and then sending it to a newspaper, you are probably wasting your time.

To begin with, newspapers want news, and since this is what they sell, your press release needs to be newsworthy. The fact that Joe Smith has replaced Tom Jones as CFO is not news. It may get picked up as filler in the local business section or trade press, but it is not the kind of information that lends itself to an article, interviews, or the front page of the Wall Street Journal. (We are continually amazed when companies come to us convinced that their piece of news belongs on the Journal's front page and that we can easily make that placement for them. That's how unrealistic expectations of PR can be.)

Even if you have a fantastic scientific product that's had proof of concept with a Fortune 100 company and you have secured $100 million in financing with a prestigious venture firm, it may not be seen as news. The truth is that other companies like yours are competing for that space. Chances are none of you will get it,

61

which is all right because there's much more to PR than writing news releases.

CRITICAL TAKEAWAY: Do not fall into the trap of focusing only on editorial publicity. That does not effectively address issues in the three-dimensional world of PR, and it puts you at risk of losing competitive advantage.

PR is the art of leveraging word of mouth and generating the buzz that creates an aura of excitement around your product or company. It can help establish you as an expert in your field through consistent media relations. If you have a parity product, it can help make yours the "cool" one compared to others. It positions you and your company as a community resource. It puts you in situations where you rub elbows with influential people able to finance your efforts or make introductions for you.

PR can be thought of as an ongoing effort to create and maintain a good relationship between a company and all of its audiences. The key is "ongoing." Given the current environment of skepticism toward corporations and the perception of them as ruthless (and occasionally dishonest) in their pursuit of profits, people have become increasingly interested in knowing about the company beyond the product. They want to know the company is morally worthy of their interest.

The public also wants to know that employees are ethical, and employees want similar reassurance about the company for which they are working.

Earned Vs. Purchased Media

Some PR, like advertising, can be purchased. This type of PR is found in many trade show programs in the form of advertorials. The trade show organizers offer participants space in the program for an "article," which the participant writes and submits. Other opportunities like this might be product placements, products included in a giveaway bag, etc.

Earned media, on the other hand, is media attention you have to work for and is not guaranteed. This type of media has more credibility because it is perceived as being reported by a neutral source and, therefore, is considered news.

What Is PR: Beyond the Press Release

PR efforts are evidenced in many different ways. If you are invited to speak at an important show or seminar, that's PR. If that event is reported in the paper, that's PR. If news happens elsewhere in your area of expertise and you are called on to explain it, that's PR. In other words, PR is what the name implies: relations with the public.

It works best when it's thought about, planned, integrated, and sustained into an overall marketing plan. No matter how well you plan, an element of unpredictability will always creep in because you cannot control the outcome.

Traditionally, PR dealt with building goodwill about a company, company-related issues, and the industry rather than selling products or services. Today, that line has significantly blurred. With the growth of event marketing and highly choreographed product marketing pushes, PR has crossed into product sales marketing and vice versa, e.g., product placement in movies and television shows, celebrity usage and cooperative partnering with compatible products. Though these are paid for, they operate as PR.

PR is often used internally as well as externally. From start-ups to Fortune 100 companies, PR's internal use is crucial to maintaining employee understanding, enthusiasm, and loyalty. Employees, officially or not, are company spokespeople.

TRUTH #6:

To get the most out of your PR, you need to establish your strategic messaging. That way, every PR effort communicates your core message in a consistent manner.

Some companies do this instinctively. They are led by managers who are out in the community, spreading the message through relationships, networking, participating in organizations and industry events, and generating and maintaining buzz about themselves and the projects and companies they are involved with. If their efforts are to be effective, other people in the company need to be behind the lead person to create follow-through with consistent messaging.

If these managers are asked to speak at a business organization, their marketing and PR people will move to maximize the situation. They may create ads to run simultaneously, give the speaker press kits to hand out, get related editorial coverage in the appropriate media, and more. In short, every effort is made to leverage the situation. The beauty of this PR effort is that it has a compounding effect, because each event helps to create more of them.

But it ain't free. Time, effort, money, focus, and commitment make it happen. The good news is that you do not have to do it overnight. Prior to all this activity, your company will have developed and agreed upon its main communications goals and how to execute them. In this way, when you or one of your managers gets an opportunity, you will know what effect you want to create, how to achieve it (because you'll have the tools to create it), and how to get the desired results.

PR is neither spontaneous nor extemporaneous, but if done well, it looks that way.

Of course, this assumes you have explored your audience and know what they need to hear to become excited by your "news" (not only what you want to say). This is where your strategic planning comes into play.

PR planning incorporates and extends your marketing planning into the corporate communications arena. The CEO and other C-level officers of the company will probably be called upon as spokespeople. This is why it is critical that the company message and strategy be thoroughly understood and consistent regardless of who is speaking. Unfortunately, for a number of reasons, what often happen is a divergence of messaging.

Too often, a company hires a PR firm and a marketing firm, and the two never meet or share insights or messaging. Instead, they develop two sets of messages. If the company's corporate communications or investor relations department also has messaging that is not in alignment with marketing or PR efforts, the company could easily have three distinct sets of communications. Since the messages are not designed to support each other, the overall message will be weakened and the company resources (speakers, money, and time) will be used less effectively.

A company must ensure its PR and marketing firms are privy to each other's work and that they share a common messaging platform. Do this, and your strategies and messages will be synchronized, and your overall communications efforts will be consistent, continuously reinforced, and strengthened with all your audiences. This is true for companies of all sizes. In short, all of these disciplines must "play nice" with each other. Turf wars will only weaken your message.

Let's assume you have done your homework and have your messaging elements. These include your positioning statement, strategy, and boilerplate copy for your press releases, logo, and tag line, along with a PR folder and printed materials to put into it.

PR Vs. Advertising

Everyone is searching for "The Answer" to their marketing woes. For decades, everyone understood and used techniques to brand their products and companies. Branding became "The Answer." Branding was the ultimate buzzword, and everyone had to hire a branding guru or agency. PR is now on the rise. Like branding, it is being touted as "The New Solution." Unfortunately, no panacea can cure all marketing woes. "The Answer" is a strategically integrated use of marketing and PR resources.

Once you have your press kit together, you will need to "flog" it to the press. This is where your PR person becomes invaluable and is why not everyone can do PR. The true art is not in the writing of press releases, though writing them is an art, but in getting the placements. Your PR person's relationships with the press are critical. A good PR person has a Rolodex with key industry contacts and has built that list over a period of years. In the process of building that list, he or she has built credibility, and therein lies the ultimate key to powerful PR: A contact will take the call from a credible PR person because the contact knows to expect the following three elements:

1. Real news that will not waste their time
2. Accurate and verifiable news
3. Background in the form of numbers, information, and people in the company to interview

That is why most PR people will tell you immediately if your story is newsworthy and how newsworthy it is. It's not just years of experience talking, but it's their relationship with their media contacts that is important. You, as a client, will go away at some point; let's face it, clients come and go. However, your PR people and their contacts will last forever. The PR people will not jeopardize that kind of relationship with shoddy information or bogus stories, because they want to make sure their call will be taken the next time. In this way, they build trust with the press and credibility, which they can, in turn, leverage to your benefit. This is true for the national press as well as industry publications and local media.

Much PR is done on the phone: tracking down editors, pitching the story to the editors, and supporting the editors in getting the information they need to get an informed article written. Company representatives, often the principals, must make themselves available for telephone calls, interviews, quotes, e-conferencing, and more.

Good PR people have a reputation and relationships that will open doors, and the company must greet the opportunity at the door with welcoming arms. Otherwise, the PR people's reputation will be tarnished, which is counter to why you hired them in the first place. More importantly, the press may feel it's been led down a dead-end path. This can result in reducing your opportunities— and may have even worse consequences.

A large hospital we know retained an experienced PR person to help it garner attention. The PR person, who had excellent credentials with the local press, convinced the feature editor of a large local paper to write a story focusing on one of the organization's areas of expertise. The PR person told the marketing manager of the organization to be available for interviews. The editor repeatedly called the manager for an interview, but the manager did not return any of the calls.

The result? The PR person had done such a good job of selling the story that the editor ran it anyway, but he featured the hospital's largest competitor. The feature article took the newspaper's entire center section and included multiple photographs of the competitor's high-tech facility, equipment, and personnel. So, when opportunity calls, return the call.

LESSON #6:
Building Your Market—The Press Pyramid

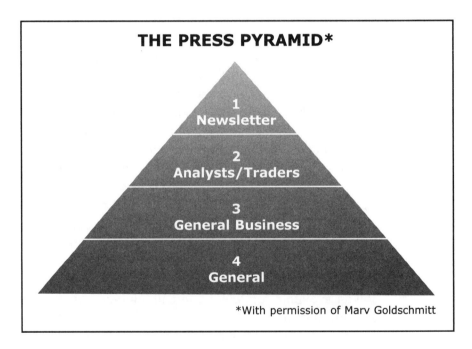

THE PRESS PYRAMID*

1
Newsletter

2
Analysts/Traders

3
General Business

4
General

*With permission of Marv Goldschmitt

The Press Pyramid represents the different levels within the press community and how they influence your audience as well as other members of the press. It also graphically depicts the size of each group and its degree of focus as well as the related economics of reaching each group.

Newsletters

By newsletters, we mean the opinion pieces and cutting-edge publications put out by thought leaders in specific industries. This smallest group, at the top of the pyramid, is the most economical to reach as well as the most knowledgeable about your science and industry. Because it is respected for its expertise, it has enormous influence. An example of a newsletter in this category is Esther Dyson's 1.0. A magazine that fits into this category is *Technology Review (MIT's Magazine of Innovation).*

These sources produce high-level information by extremely knowledgeable people who tend to be ahead of the curve and actively seek out newsworthy technologies in your industry. These people are the ones who often identify the next new trend and tout it to their readers. Because of their knowledge, others in the industry seek out their opinions, and they are often asked to speak about topics related to their expertise. Because these people are so focused, being covered in one of their newsletters can efficiently deliver your message and, thus, have wonderful consequences for you.

Analysts/Traders

In this next level of influence, analysts and traders speak to the investment market and your customer base. The people in organizations such as META, Gartner, and Forrester put out highly regarded reports, research market evaluations, and stock market predictions, which can influence investors, your stock price, and the value of your IPO stock. And these people will ultimately be purchasing your science, product, or service as direct customers, stockholders, or investors. Included in this category are blogs, such as Network World (www.networkworld.com). Catching their attention will yield significant results in moving your company/technology forward.

General Business

The third tier of the Press Pyramid consists of the general business media, such as *Business Week* and CNBC. Science and business reporters in all media will look up the pyramid for newsworthy angles, the latest trends, and background about a particular area/industry they are covering.

General

The fourth tier of the Press Pyramid is the general press, which looks up to the entire pyramid for its background information and validation of your information; however, this group also generates some original information. They have a voracious appetite for business news with an interesting enough slant and appeal to the large audiences they serve (the general population).

All of the pyramid categories are open to being pitched by you or your PR representatives. Obviously, the further down the pyramid you go, the more expensive it becomes to reach them. Many more media venues and, thus, more people have to be reached. More competition exists for their attention, and their audience is larger and more diffuse.

Ideally, an effective and efficient PR campaign would reach out to the newsletters first and rely on their spreading the word about you down the pyramid. This is particularly important for start-ups that cannot afford to go after the entire pyramid. Your "elevator messaging" will often find its way into use as a sound bite. This is why your messaging is important: People on the pyramid will often be communicating about you without you being there and will refer to the messaging in how they portray you. This is also why your messaging must be consistent.

Members of the press will refer to your press releases, brochures, and web site to get the information they need about you before they contact you. If your messaging is scattered, unclear, and inconsistent, the newsworthiness of your company's efforts may be lost, and you could lose a great opportunity.

Critical Takeaway: If you are just looking for a one-month or two-month PR "fix," save your money. That's barely enough time to get you on the radar of certain audiences and not enough to have any kind of real effect. Usually, to have a meaningful impact, a PR campaign or effort should run a minimum of six consecutive months because building momentum takes a long time.

Putting Public Relations to Work

To generate effective PR, every company, regardless of budget, industry, or size, needs to have these basics in place. You can do these yourself or hire a PR or marketing firm to do them for you:

- Registered name of company: Ideally, this will be a memorable name that will help you stand apart.

- Logo: Make sure it has legs so it will last five to ten years and will reproduce easily in all formats. One key test is how your logo will fax in black and white.

- Folder with two pockets: This is a flexible, all-purpose holder that has your branding on it.

- Tag line/commanding claim: This gives people a tiny handle, or an image, to help remember you.

- Descriptor line: This is used when the name of the company and the tag line do not adequately describe the service or product.

- Messaging: This consists of short phrases or sentences that quickly and clearly position your company and/or products in the marketplace. Included in your messaging is your boilerplate copy, a short paragraph that factually describes your company. You usually see this at the end of every press release.

Hiring A PR Firm

A number of factors enter into this decision. As with anything else, you want to ask your business colleagues who they are using and if they feel good enough about a firm to refer them. Is your product so complex that it needs somebody with a certain expertise who can talk about it intelligently to the press? Have you determined a budget or do you have a good idea of how much money you are willing to spend?

Here are ten key questions to ask when interviewing PR candidates:

1. How long have they been in business?

2. Are the businesses they represent similar to yours? (Do they specialize in an industry sector?)

3. How long have their current clients been with them? Can you talk to some of these clients?

4. Can they show you a portfolio of articles, placements, and coverage they have generated?

5. Who will be handling your account on a daily basis? Make sure you meet them. What is their background, and how long have they been with the company? How flexible are they? Can they turn on a dime and help you take advantage of sudden opportunities?

6. How will the relationship be structured? Will they work on a retainer or project basis? How much will it cost? Does that include a clipping service? If not, what will the additional costs be for clipping services, etc.?

7. How often and in what form will they report their activities to you?

8. What services can you expect for your money? In what time frame?

9. What are their media contacts (in each of the levels of the pyramid)? Do they specialize in a particular kind of media?

10. If need be, what are the terms for disengaging their services?

Large Firms Vs. Small Firms

Larger firms may be well-known and have a good reputation. They may even have a famous name you would like to drop in the hopes of impressing others. However, they also have a larger infrastructure to support and, thus, a higher threshold of billing. Moreover, the president, or senior manager of the firm, whom you might meet at the first presentation, is almost certainly not going to work on your small account. A smaller firm is usually hungrier, and its senior management (often trained at the larger firms) is more likely to work directly on your account.

Perhaps one of the most important qualities in hiring a PR vendor is chemistry and trust in the specific person who will be working with you. You will have to work closely with, and feel comfortable with, the person who will be representing your company to the public. Sometimes, these two factors are more important than all the others.

Case History: Healthcare Technologies

Healthcare Technologies wanted some PR done. Since they had no marketing plan, they did not know where they fit into the market. All their messaging was focused on the benefits of their software product, MediScribe (a medical transcription product). Unfortunately, their benefits were identical to their competition's, so this tactic was not enough to get them more market share. However, when they did demonstrate their product in front of prospective customers, 80 percent of the time they won the business. The problem was they did not get enough invitations to pitch their software.

The company needed to understand the market better and know how to differentiate itself. A market analysis done by its PR firm showed that the company had technical expertise that differentiated it from the competition. Using this knowledge, the PR company recommended repositioning the company from a full-service provider to a technical leader.

To increase the company's number of qualified leads, the PR agency developed a challenge called "Take the MediScribe challenge!" A donation to a charity would be made in exchange for the prospective customer trying the product. This became the new theme, and the product differentiators were then wrapped around it.

The web site's home page was updated to reflect the new theme and invited people to take the challenge. This is just one example of how the new messaging was delivered to the company's audience. Now when PR and marketing communications were done, Healthcare Technologies had a consistent campaign to tie all their messaging together. The takeaway for prospects was, "We are so confident about our product that we'll put our money where our mouth is," and that is a powerful message in any industry.

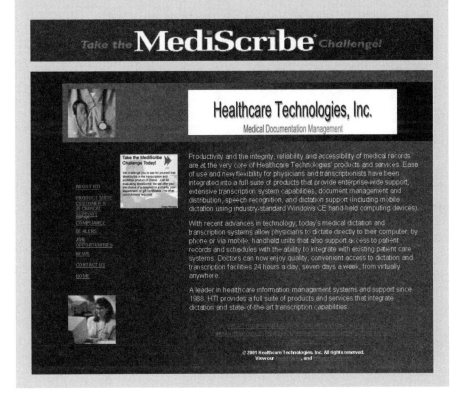

So, Can You Do PR First?

If you mean, "Can I do my PR first before I do advertising or other marketing?" the answer is yes. However, keep these points in mind:

- You need to think about your messaging/branding first, including establishing long-term and short-term goals.

- If you do PR before you do your web site, people will have nowhere to go to check you out and get more of your company's information.

- You need stationery, business cards, and a folder to put together a professional-looking press kit.

If you are doing PR first because you think it's the cheaper way to go, you will still need to spend time and money for it to be effective. The more time you spend up front, the more efficient your PR efforts will be.

Lie #7

I Know How to Market
(A few words of wisdom to the Scientific Founder.)

"The first thing we look for is the quality of the management team and those teams that understand the difference between a science project and a plan to build a substantial company. The best teams are able to adjust their strategies that address the ever-changing nature of the industry."

Dennis J. Purcell,
Senior Managing Director, Aisling Capital LLC

Another title for this chapter could be "I invented this product, and no one else is qualified to market it." When was the last time you heard a line that encompassed this much BS in one short sentence? Yet this kind of arrogance is understandable coming from someone whose life has been consumed by studying and developing a new product, process, or service. The pride of ownership is evident.

So is the blindness.

The emotional parallel is similar to raising a child and having to step back and allow the child to go out into the world. Sooner or later the parent has to detach. Wise parents recognize when the time to step back has come and to turn their baby over to others whose expertise will carry the child along. The parent remains on the team, supporting and encouraging when necessary.

And so should a wise inventor, a company founder, or a scientific CEO.

Too often, despite considerable knowledge, scientific leaders of a company do not know the first thing about business or marketing. Nor is there any reason why they should. They have not made this part of their learning curve. Their assumption seems to be, "If you don't need a Ph.D. to do it, how hard can it be?" So they are often surprised to find it more complex and critical than they had assumed.

People in the venture community know that if the scientific leader cannot let go of control of all processes in the company, he or she is often looking at failure.

In the post dot and bio bomb environments, the funding community is less likely to take a chance on a lone scientist or entrepreneur with a good idea. In fact, most of the business community will not take a start-up seriously unless they see a management team in place. Often, the management team is built around a CEO with a business background and the scientific founder or lead entrepreneur. VCs have a preference for management team members who have already brought a start-up to fruition.

In fact, VCs and investment bankers know that management is the most important part of a company. Weak science or a weak idea does not mean a company's end. A good management team should be flexible and must parlay the "weakness" into consulting or some other workable option. Conversely, good science or a strong idea does not mean a company's automatic success. A weak management team can kill the "good" science or strong idea so it never sees the light of day.

By weak, we mean a team with no true marketing, business, or sales background.

In short, the best way to move your company forward is to bring in marketing and business professionals who are as expert in their areas as you are in the science. This frees you to manage the development of the product or process and to prepare it for the market. Simultaneously, your marketing pros will be preparing it for the marketplace while your business people are lining up the venture money to support bringing the product to market.

Use Your Unseen Network

VCs, PR firms, accountants, marketing firms, lawyers, and insurance companies network together and talk to each other. At any point in developing your product, they can make connections for you. Your marketing firm may know sources of money, your VC may know a good PR firm, and your lawyer may know a good accountant. People who work with start-ups often have unique relationships that can benefit you. If you are a first-time start-up, many of the issues and problems may be new to you.

By using these relationships you are accessing a core network that can bring years of expertise to your project. But you must reach out and tell them you are having a problem or need a resource in some area. Often, they will not volunteer information for fear of overstepping the role for which you hired them. You have to communicate your needs.

By involving them early in the process, you can put your time to more profitable use. While you are busy finalizing the product and raising venture capital, their knowledge of the technology can help you champion it to the marketplace.

TRUTH #7:

Eventually, to ensure your product's success, you have to bring in a team with the necessary expertise to launch it. The earlier you do this, the better your company's chances of success.

Case History

A board-certified physician decided to start his own dietary supplements company. He had special expertise in this area and developed several products. He wrote several books discussing the nature of the conditions or deficiencies and how his supplements corrected them. This was a good way to launch his company. Theoretically, the books would aid in establishing him as an authority while also helping to sell the product. He was astute enough to know to hire marketing and business managers, and he wanted to bring in outside marketing, strategic, and web support.

Unfortunately, each time these knowledgeable experts tried to do the job he hired them for, he would not relinquish control. He could not loosen his hold on the product, funding, or planning. Because of this, the experts were unable to help him take his company to the next step. Consequently, he still runs the company like a mom-and-pop operation using his family members to fill mail orders on weekends. Other entrepreneurs, selling similar products, have done their marketing homework and have become extremely successful.

So, Do You Know How to Market?

Of course you do, just as everyone who's taken high school biology can start a scientific company—meaning "of course not." Marketing and development take years of training. Stick with your true expertise and bring in others to work with your baby to help it grow.

Lie #8

I Have a Business Plan; I Don't Need a Marketing Plan

"Often overlooked is the value of the actual strategic marketing development and tactical planning process that can uncover opportunities for product refinement and improvement, thus ultimately improving your product's launch and break-even time."

Joan Rose,
Assistant Dean for Communications at Penn Law
(University of Pennsylvania Law School)

It would be nice if it worked this way. Unfortunately, a business plan is not a marketing plan, and using one as such could wind up costing you dearly in time, money, and missed opportunities.

Business plans give a more global view of a company. They speak to the company's goals, explain its products and services, describe its business pitch, discuss the company's management team and its expertise, and give a detailed plan of how it will finance itself. A good business plan will also give a brief overview of the company's need for marketing and how it will be utilized.

The marketing plan is a spin-off of the marketing overview. It drills down through all the issues of getting a communications and sales program launched. It stands apart from the business plan as a separate entity and serves as a highly detailed blueprint or road map of how you plan to reach customers.

The plan lays out your goals and tactics, the tactics' timeframe, how the costs of these elements fit into your budget, and how you will use them to achieve your marketing goals. Importantly, it defines pricing.

So, what's the difference between a business plan and a marketing plan?

Take a look at these charts. They outline a typical business plan and a typical marketing plan. You can see activities and analyses that are important to a marketing plan but are absent from the business plan.

BUSINESS PLAN
1. Executive Summary
2. Company Description
3. Industry Analysis
4. Competitive Analysis
5. Market Segmentation
6. Marketing and Sales
7. Management, Organization, and Integration
8. Operations
9. Business Risks
10. Balanced Scorecard
11. Financials

Now take item #6 on the chart and drill down to create your marketing plan.

6. Marketing and Sales a. Marketing Plan
1. How do we define our business?
2. What is our vision, and what are our objectives?
3. What are our markets?
4. Currently, who are our largest clients (if any)?
5. Who are our target clients? a. Why are they our targets? b. What is our sales approach?
6. Who is our competition?
7. How are we different from the competition?
8. Where do we fit in the marketplace? What is our value to our customer?
9. What is our growth strategy?
10. What are our partnerships (if any)?
11. What kind of market research will we do (If any)?
12. What are our marketing goals and objectives?
13. How will we promote and advertise ourselves?

Each item on the marketing plan has its own detailed drill-down that is even more removed from the business plan. For instance, take point 13 on the marketing plan, for promotion and advertising, and see how much depth of detail that one aspect covers.

Promotion Plan	Issues	Notes and Drill-Downs
Strategy	Vertical markets vs. horizontal markets	Will we be selling to a single business category or to many?
Market Position	High-end, mid-range, low-end	In a line-up of comparable products and companies arranged by image, quality, or cost, where do we fit? Is that where we want to be?
Corporate Branding/Identity	Do we need a logo, stationery, pocket folder, brochure, web site, or basic messaging?	How will we accomplish this and how soon?
Communications Tactics	**Collateral**: Will we need product brochures, technical briefs, individual product sell sheets, direct mail campaign, or special events announcements? **PR**: Will we need press releases, white papers, industry coverage, speaking engagements, special events, infomercials, or video news releases? **Web Site**: How will we use our web site? Will we use it as an online brochure or e-commerce site? Will we offer corporate giveaways, promotions, etc.? **Media**: Will we use print, TV, radio, outdoor (billboard, transit), interactive media, industry-specific alerts, newsletters, or trade show opportunities? **Trade Shows**: Will we use convention panels, invitations, printed handouts, giveaways, or hospitality suites?	How much do we have to spend? What is our budget? Which of these do we want to use and why? Can we afford this all at once, or do we need to be selective? How long will our informational materials remain current? How will our various tactics and efforts interact and support each other? What time frames are we dealing with? Can we meet them?

Drilling down opens up more issues to be addressed. At this point, we are far removed from your business plan and well on the way to creating an actionable plan for launching your product or company.

You must decide how much detail you want, but even if you spend only an hour scribbling out a marketing plan on a napkin, you will have a better handle on how you are going to enter the marketplace and how much you will spend. At the least, we recommend you not go out into the world without the three basic branding elements: a logo, a tag line, and a pocket folder with your logo and tag line printed on it.

Defining Your Marketing Objectives

Let's assume you have your business plan in place. Now, how do you define your marketing plan? The first step is to figure out who you are, where you fit in the marketplace, and how you are going to leverage your position to make sales.

A number of methodologies can be used for this. One of the most common and most easily implemented is called the SWOT analysis. SWOT stands for Strengths, Weaknesses, Opportunities, and Threats.

The SWOT Analysis

Though you may feel you know all these answers in your head, there's nothing like listing out the hard cold truth on paper to help you look at your product and its place in the marketplace realistically. To ensure a true perspective on your market and eliminate the natural bias of one person's vision, we recommend that you do this with a small group of colleagues who understand your business/product.

Take a sheet of paper and divide it into four sections: Strengths, Weaknesses, Opportunities, and Threats. List everything you know about the product in its proper category. If you put an item in one category, it cannot go in another unless you reword it. Suppose you are the sole proprietor of a company, which is a strength and weakness. Here's an example of how it might be listed in your SWOT analysis:

Strengths: As a sole proprietor, you are the go-to person with the most expertise. Your clients know that when they call, they will always get you. When they give your company an order or an assignment, you will be the one working on it, or at the very least, the one personally reviewing it prior to leaving your company. When they sign on with your company, they get you.

Weaknesses: As a sole proprietor, you can only service a limited number of clients or customers. Your business size may be limited because you are either doing the actual work or reviewing the work being done by your colleagues. Therefore, you cannot compete for some of the larger, sometimes more important, glamorous, and more remunerative business in your category

Once you have filled out the Strengths and Weaknesses sections, move on to the Opportunities and Threats sections. The important thing is to get it all out of your head and onto the paper. Often, you will find that when you examine the Threats in this fashion, you will find an Opportunity hiding in the details.

approach). Therefore, if you have a good year, you will spend more money on marketing. However, if you have a bad year, you will spend less. Even though this sounds reasonable in theory, this approach is flawed. In a bad year, you should probably increase your marketing to drive more sales and not adjust downward, which will almost guarantee fewer sales.

5. *The zero-based budgeting approach:* This approach means you start each year with a blank slate and determine your marketing budget based on projected costs and revenues. In this approach, you must justify every line item. This puts you on the line to deliver, so that at any point during the year, you know what your score is.

Is It Sales or Is It Marketing?

Do not confuse sales with marketing. Marketing is the process of defining your pricing and distribution, planning your promotional efforts, and executing these in a way that results in sales. Marketing positions you in the marketplace, promotes the product to your audience, and ideally resonates with them on an emotional level. Marketing creates you as a desirable entity in your marketplace and predisposes the customer to select your product over others.

Sales is about getting on the phone or otherwise getting in front of potential customers and selling the product. Sales is the physical act that uses the messages and materials that the marketing plan has defined and developed. Though the materials can create awareness and generate leads, only the salesperson can move on the leads and close the deal.

In a nutshell, marketing attracts, and sales closes.

These two functions are sister functions within the company, but each requires a different skill set to move the company forward. Some lucky companies have one person with enough perspective to manage them both, but most companies do not. Salespeople

---

Like Computers, Marketing Programs Are a Necessary Business Tool

Marketing is not just about return on investment (ROI). Marketing is about building your marketplace brand name and image. This recognition will lead back to sales but not as a quid pro quo proposition that results in immediate payback. Rather, this cumulative process develops increasing returns over time. This is why you should think about marketing in terms of an investment, like good computers and lab equipment.

know how to approach the different customers, how to manage leads, how to work the trade shows, and how to close the deal. In fact, good salespeople have a unique talent that makes people want to buy from them. Many can almost sell anything. On the other hand, marketing people need to have a more global perspective, such as where the product is in its development cycle, what new features may be coming, and what new competition may be on the horizon.

Marketing needs to juggle all the different aspects of the marketing program by standardizing messages to multiple audiences and executing various materials over a long period. Marketing is responsible for ensuring that the branding and the messaging stays consistent. Marketing ensures that the sales team has the support it needs to move people from being prospects to customers.

For these reasons, we suggest you separate the two functions by hiring a different person for each job.

Case Study: You!

You are the star of this case study. Spend some time filling out the following charts using your company as an example. Even if your time is limited, you will quickly see that you need to think seriously about a number of aspects that have to do with launching your product/company.

SWOT ANALYSIS—WORKSHEET	
Strengths	Weaknesses
Opportunities	Threats

MARKETING PLAN WORKSHEET

1. How do we define our business?

2. What is our vision, and what are our objectives?

3. What are our markets?

4. Currently, who are our largest clients (if any)?

5. Who are our target clients?

    a. Why are they our targets?

    b. What is our sales approach?

6. Who is our competition?

7. How are we different from the competition?

8. Where do we fit in the marketplace?

    What is our value to our customer?

9. What is our growth strategy?

10. What are our partnerships (if any)?

PROMOTION PLAN WORKSHEET	Issues
Is our strategy vertical markets, horizontal markets, or both?	
Is our market position high-end, mid-range, or low-end?	
Are our corporate branding/identity elements in place?	
Do we need a logo?	
Do we need stationery?	
Do we need a pocket folder?	
Do we need business cards?	
Do we need basic messaging?	
Are our communications tactics in place? What do we need? What is the budget?	
Web Site: How will we use it? Will we use it as an online brochure or an e-commerce site? Will we offer corporate give-aways, catalog, promotions, etc.?	
Collateral	
Product brochures	
Technical briefs	
Individual product sell sheets	
Direct mail campaign	
Special events material	
Video (Sales? Training? Demo?)	
Invites/announcements	
Public Relations	
Press releases	
White papers	
Industry coverage	
Speaking engagements	
Special events	
Infomercial	
Video news releases	
Media to Use:	
Print	
TV	
Radio	

PROMOTION PLAN WORKSHEET	Issues
Outdoor (billboard, transit, etc.)	
Interactive: e-mails, etc.	
Industry-specific alerts	
Newsletters	
Trade Shows	
Booth, panels, etc.	
Program ads	
Invitations	
Printed handouts	
Giveaways	
Hospitality suites	
How much time do we have until the first show?	

Now here is the big nasty. You must create a timeline of when materials need to be finished. You'll have to be aware of the following time frames:

1. A brochure or pocket folder will need ten working days to print, not including shipping time. A trade show booth takes four weeks to produce and ship, and this does not include creating the physical booth. (We are only talking about the graphics.) Now do we have your attention?

2. Your agency will need a minimum of three weeks to create the brochure and get your approval for it. This assumes your approval process is quick and your direction has been succinct. This also supposes you have your logo, business cards, and messaging ready.

3. Trade shows often need to be booked months, and sometimes a year, in advance. If you want an ad in the trade show program, you will need to reserve space months in advance. If you want to produce and send a postcard announcing that you will be at the trade show, you need a minimum of three full weeks to produce the card (including creating, approving, printing, and mailing it).

4. For advertising placements, a magazine generally wants your ad at least four to six weeks prior to publication. Radio and TV placement times vary and need to be checked when you do

your media plan. (You need to do a media plan if you are going to put multiple ads in multiple places.) Web site banner ads come in different sizes, and different web sites have different technical requirements. Their timing also varies depending on the site where you want to place your ad.

Being aware of timelines for producing your materials is important and can seem complex but is as easy as any project that requires good project management to pull off. Creating a timeline by working backward from your due dates will keep you on schedule. The timeline might even scare the pants off your company management when it sees how long communications materials can take to produce. This kind of chart works well, and you can expand it to handle multiple projects and the steps it takes to complete them. Here's a sample covering a brochure and trade show booth panels:

PROJECT & TASKS	MONTH: October																						
	1	2	3	4	5	6	7	8	9	10	11	12	13	14	15	16	17	18	19	20	21	22	23
Brochure																							
Layout	█	█	█	█	█	█	█																
Copy	█	█	█	█	█																		
Approvals			█	█	█																		
Pre-press							█	█															
Printing										█	█	█	█	█	█	█	█	█	█				
Shipping																					█	█	
Booth Panels																							
Design	█	█	█	█																			
Approvals			█	█																			
Printing						█	█	█	█	█	█	█	█	█	█	█	█	█	█				
Shipping																				█	█	█	
Due at Trade Show																							█

This is clearly an aggressive schedule that makes no concessions for weekends or slip-ups, and we advise taking more time. If you were also doing a "save the date" postcard/invite or placing an ad in the trade show program, you would need a longer time frame.

So, Do You Need a Marketing Plan If You Have Your Business Plan?

The more detailed the marketing plan is, the better for you. Even an informal plan will keep you on track and give you a reason why you should and should not spend money on various marketing tactics. Your business plan cannot achieve this alone nor should it be expected to.

Lie #9

Only a Technical Person Can Market My Product

"Nobody buys a product because of how it works. Even technical people buy a product because of what it does for them. What problem does it solve, how does it make them feel. Nail that, and communicate it, and you've got a sale."

Frank DeVito,
Partner and President, DeVito Fitterman Advertising

Let's get this straight: You would rather trust your marketing to someone who has never done a full-scale marketing plan? Someone who has no experience in translating "tech talk" into product benefits in "people talk"? A lot of technical people have this notion, which is why trade shows are full of badly conceived, boring marketing materials that obscure a product's true brilliance. Just because someone has a Ph.D. does not mean he or she knows how to distill your product's benefits into an effective message that quickly resonates with your market.

Even the simplest piece of your marketing communications program may require hours of experienced effort to produce.

We know of one technical entrepreneur who carefully created what he was convinced was the perfect one-sentence "elevator pitch" for his new IT process. It went like this: "Have you got 30 or 40 minutes so I can show you my slide show?" If you cannot communicate the value of your company or product quickly, no one is going to give you the time. Can your tech guy distill your company or product benefits into an effective 30-second elevator speech?

Here's another example of a knowledgeable technical person's take on marketing. The chief technology officer of a company designated himself as the company spokesperson at trade shows and marketing fairs. His feeling was that he could best explain the science. And he could. However, the only people who understood him were the other Ph.D.s, and they were not his primary product purchasers. He came back from each experience thinking he was a success, and he was because the other Ph.D.s loved him. But he wasn't making any sales. In fact, he was inadvertently building his own image at the company's expense.

We also know an off-shore scientist who would go in front of venture capitalist (VC) audiences at boot camps and regale them for hours about the details of how his science worked. But he could not answer simple questions, like "What are the applications for this technology?" and "Why should a company purchase your product?" He was an expert at raising money for research but a flop when it came to commercializing the science into a profitable technology. Do these stories sound familiar? They should. There are tons of them out there. Consider them warning signs about what not to do.

To put it another way, ask a scientist to tell you the time, and he'll tell you how to build a clock.

All too often, scientific founders, inventors, and other highly trained entrepreneurs assume that only they can do the marketing because nobody understands the product as they do. They assume nobody can do the business and fundraising except them because no one else can understand the importance of what they have created. This inability to make the leap between invention and marketing is one of the primary reasons technology start-ups fail.

The feelings are understandable. This is their baby, but like any child, it must be allowed to go out into the world. Sooner or later, the scientist or inventor must take a back seat to business professionals and let the baby go out so others can commercialize it.

In short, you cannot be so in love with your science, invention, or product improvement that your ardor (which often comes across as arrogance) gets in the way of its success. In the same way you know your science, other trained professionals know marketing.

TRUTH #9:

Even if you are just marketing to others like yourself, your technology needs to be translated into benefits that your entire market can grasp quickly and act on.

Here are some things that a good marketing professional can do that you might not be able to do or should not waste your time trying to learn:

- Uncover and describe in easily understood terms what your science or product does
- Quickly articulate the benefit to the user
- Differentiate your science from its competition
- Position it as the "best choice" to the end user
- Communicate an understanding of your proprietary science and its market value to such varied groups as VCs, market analysts, the press, potential customers, and potential mom-and-pop investors, without talking down to one group or over the heads of another
- Present your messaging consistently over time, through different vehicles, and to different audiences
- Make the most of your product without overselling or misrepresenting it
- Develop an elevator pitch that allows you to communicate your company's uniqueness quickly, succinctly, and consistently
- Explain glitches in your product or process and how you plan to deal with them. People will find out, and if you tell them now, it will add credibility to you, your product, and your company

CRITICAL TAKEAWAY: Many marketing and promotional professionals have experience with technical products in scientific markets. More importantly, professional marketers know how to distill a product, even a complex one, into an effective promotional message. The marketing fundamentals are the same no matter what the product.

LESSON #9:

The best person to market your product is the one best able to understand and explain it. He or she is able to communicate your product's value to all target audiences. Ideally, this should be someone from the outside. By working with an outsider, you are more likely to get new market perspectives about your product. Look for someone like a marketing consultant or marketing agency with a track record of successful product launches.

Where do you find this kind of success? Start by asking others in your field who have faced the same challenge. You will probably learn as much from talking to those with bad experiences as those with positive experiences. Ask those with successful launches to recommend their resources. Interview five or six, and select three to bid on your project. Let them know they are in a competitive bidding situation, and you want each to bid on the same specs—for instance, a logo design, a brochure, and an ad for a trade show program book.

Though this process takes time, it will be time well spent. You will gain a better understanding of the challenges you face, the kinds of resources you feel comfortable with, and the cost.

Case History: Synthon Chiragenics

Synthon Chiragenics—Before

The scientific founder of Synthon is a world-renowned expert on carbohydrates and chiral chemistry. When he founded the company, he knew he needed a folder for his sales materials and other printed pieces. He was adept in drug design programming, so he "drew" a carbohydrate molecule and showed its chirality or "handedness" by creating a graphic that represented a mirror image. This was a literal execution of a sophisticated concept. He chose to create a building block graphic, which became the company logo, to show that the company makes drug building blocks (again, a literal approach). At the time, in the mid-1990s, black was the big color in biotech, so he chose a black background for most of the promotional materials. He kept the looks fairly consistent. The tag line (or benefit or promise) was "Chirality from nature."

All the correct efforts were put forth in creating promotional materials. But the materials were improperly designed: The graphics just floated unconnected on the page and, though they had meaning, the meaning was lost in the presentation. The tag line or commanding claim merely stated that the company got its chiral entities from nature.

This is a typical, albeit highly sophisticated, version of a start-up's marketing efforts.

Fortunately, this founder had the smarts to know that he could not do this all himself. He knew he needed to bring in a CEO as bright as he was to take care of the business side, to raise capital, and to bring the company to market. He also knew that, after bringing in the CEO, he needed to relinquish control so marketing professionals could promote the company.

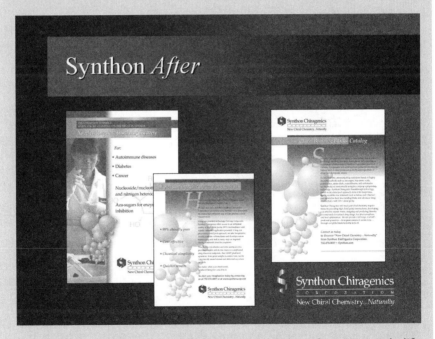

Here's the "professional" result: The identification and differentiation separate Synthon from the pack of biotechs in its niche while creating an entire corporate identity program that extends into every marketing piece.

The logo was changed from a building block to a six-sided carbohydrate molecule with a ribbon graphic running through the center. The ribbon represents the molecule's chiral halves. The ribbon looked like the letter "S" and, thus, reflects the Synthon name. The new commanding claim did a better job than "chirality from nature" at positing the company's true points of differentiation. "New chiral chemistry...naturally" gives the benefit of discovering new chiral entities for drug development purposes from nature, meaning from naturally occurring carbohydrates. The commanding claim meant something more to potential purchasers of their products, since it suggested they could create new chiral compounds, shorten steps in conventional drug production, and effectively enable new drug discovery that had been prohibitively expensive before.

The revamped materials reflected the company's evolution from a start-up to a grownup. The company was a serious player in the marketplace, and its new look accurately portrayed its status as a growing, reputable, more mature company in its corner of the biotech universe.

Convention materials and a product catalog were also created using the new look. At the first professional meeting where these materials appeared, they were greeted with kudos from the company's investors as well as from the company's competitors.

So, Is a Technical Person the Best Choice to Be Your Marketing Guru?

If your goal is to give your product the best possible start, probably not. Marketing fundamentals are the same no matter what the product. So, look around for a marketing company that has a good track record with a range of products as well as experience working with technology companies.

Do Not Expect Instant Marketing

Building a good marketing program will still require your time as the marketing people get up to speed on the product. The marketing materials shown to you on the first round will still be rough drafts, though they have been computer-generated and look finished. They need refinement and sometimes redirection to become tight and focused. This back and forth helps you and your marketing partner form a strong bond. And as time goes by, it will require less and less effort on your part.

To make sure the marketing company understands your product, assign a contact person to work with the company, someone who has the time and patience to explain the product and brainstorm about possible marketing avenues to explore. Make sure you and the marketing company agree on your needs and timetable. And do not jump to produce marketing materials until you have developed your basic messaging platform.

Lie #10

I Can Get the Work Done Cheaper

"If cost is your only measuring stick, then you're going to fail. And if you're going to fail, spend very little on your marketing. Success has a price, and it's always more than you think."

Joe Bergmann,
Marketing Strategist, Interactive Creative Director

Yes, you probably can. The question is, exactly what are you getting for less? Another question is, why do you need to get it cheaper?

Are you simply being a good steward of your company's resources, are you resistant to doing marketing (unsure of its value), or are you being pressured by others in the company? If you are conserving your company's resources, be sure that in comparing pricing, you are comparing services, value, etc. In other words, make sure you are comparing apples to apples and oranges to oranges.

As some of the following stories will show, the "vendors" you choose to work with to create your marketing materials may have varying degrees of marketing expertise in addition to their specific skill sets. You may find a young designer who can quickly assemble some attractive sell sheets or a simple brochure (perhaps you had a rush deadline so the materials would be available for a trade show). But if the work does not reflect your company's overall positioning, strategy, and branding, you may find yourself wishing you had not jumped so quickly to a solution or had such a knee-jerk reaction to a deadline or a cheaper price.

On the other hand, your resistance may be justified. For instance, a nanotech company we know had two vendors pitching it for a project that included web site enhancement, minor logo changes, and public relations.

One vendor was small and had been highly recommended by someone on the board of directors and a C-level executive within the company. The other vendor had been around for many years and had a well-established reputation. The first was a marketing company, and the second was a PR company. Both had deep expertise in this company's market.

The client's product was a highly effective component part for manufacturers of a larger piece of high-tech equipment. Their component significantly increased this equipment's performance.

The client chose to go with the larger PR company, for two reasons:

1. The PR company had another client who was a potential user of the component, and the client assumed the PR company would make introductions to this potential user.
2. The client wanted the glamour associated with using a large, well-known PR company (though the client would never admit this).

We know working with a glamour agency can satisfy one's ego. But this approach is not always productive and can waste money.

The larger PR firm also had a reputation for overcharging. The client spoke to the firm about the cost issue and felt assured he could control it.

Three months later, word got out that only one press release had been written and issued, and related promotional efforts brought in exactly one phone call from a potential customer (another client of the PR firm who probably made the call as a courtesy to the agency). For this, the client was billed approximately $35,000. After some irate conversations, the bill was cut to $17,000, which remains a high fee for a single, unproductive press release.

Interestingly, $35,000 was the same fee proposed by the smaller company for a wider range of PR services, including three months of the following services:

• writing multiple press releases
• researching placement opportunities
• pitching the releases to various editors
• getting the releases placed with magazines
• creating a press book showing all articles that had been placed

This example shows what commonly happens to start-up companies when they get caught up in the glamour of working with a big-time PR or marketing firm without considering their real needs and resources and the results they are looking to achieve. This example

When Bigger May Not Be Better

One of the draws of going with a top agency is the assumption that you will be working with people who have a bigger vision of your product's possibilities and potential than you have.

This is not always the case. Top agencies come with top prices and do not always assign top people to lower-budget jobs. If you choose to go this way, be specific that you want to meet the team who will be doing your work and with whom you will interface. If you do not, you may wind up paying higher prices for a junior team with less experience.

also shows the hidden costs that often come with using a larger agency.

Here is another story: A start-up client had a trusted marketing firm working on his logo, brochure, PR fact sheets, data sheet, signage, packaging, and other key branding elements. When it came time to do the web site, however, the client chose to use the CEO's young nephew, who had recently graduated from an Ivy League college where he had learned programming.

The assumption was that the company would save some money while getting the benefit of a technical person knowledgeable in the latest programming techniques. In addition, the young relative would be getting a leg up on his career. Sounds like a win-win situation, right?

Unfortunately not. While the programmer was given the company's new logo and tag line, he had no clue about marketing. So the web site did not reflect correct usage of the branding elements being developed by the marketing company and did not accommodate the copy platforms or product information. More importantly, no thought was given to the web site's information flow (called information architecture) and how it should work together with the site graphics, which were haphazardly chosen and poorly used.

A programmer is a programmer. Even a good programmer is not an art director, a graphic designer, a copywriter, a communicator, an information architect, or a marketing strategist. In this case, since the programmer was fresh out of school, he also had no business experience.

The result? A month after the site went up, the marketing company was called in to redo the site. The company lost some money in the process, and it lost time in getting its image out to the public.

Here's another example: An IT company was preparing for its initial public offering (IPO). The marketing company had completed a beautiful color brochure with folder and sell sheets that reflected revised branding elements. The company had designers and programmers on staff, but they were offshore. The CEO was toying with the idea of assigning the web site to his in-house/offshore staff. In fact, while the agency was meeting with the client and its web design was on the table, an e-mail came in from the offshore team with a design for the web site, which the CEO quickly slapped onto the table next to the agency's design.

The comparison was fatal.

The offshore team clearly had no understanding of the marketing issues, the nature of the assignment, or the intended audience. The CEO's face instantly acknowledged that the in-house/offshore option would not work. This was a sign of a truly intelligent CEO, who reversed his own decision for the company's good, and he did it in front of his own people and his ad agency. As a result, his web site accurately reflected his company and was uploaded in time for the company's IPO.

> ### Don't Get Blinded by a Flashy Look
>
> A hot young design team may have work that looks hip, but you need to ask yourself if they understand marketing, your marketing needs, and your product. Do they have the wisdom you need to interpret your direction and execute it in a manner that communicates? (A flashy look does not always communicate. Sometimes, it's just cool to look at and tends to sell the designers when it should be selling your product.)

Entrepreneurs, C-level executives, and managers (who are experts in their field) can easily assume that marketing can't be all that difficult. And it is not, but it is a skill requiring experience to execute properly. Marketing consumes a lot of time and requires a great deal of attention to details that may not be obvious to the uninitiated eye. Marketing does not follow traditional scientific rules where you can predict an outcome and follow a course to achieve it. It is more of an art or craft and requires flexibility, agility, and long-range planning as well as the ability to visualize long-range results when undertaking a course of action.

So, by all means, be aware of costs, but factor in value, too. What are you getting in return for your money? Consider your time. How much time can you put against your marketing? How much time do you want to spend on marketing?

CRITICAL TAKEAWAY: Regardless of your budget, find professionals with solid skills to get the best bang for your buck. They should have experience and vision, particularly marketing experience and strategic savvy. These people should understand where a simple fact sheet fits into the bigger picture of your marketing sales structure and your branding needs.

You also want chemistry between you and the professionals. You need to feel comfortable that they can listen and are hearing what you might not be able to articulate fully. In short, you want them to hear, see, and understand your overall marketing issues. People who can do this will be able to shepherd your marketing efforts and will become valuable team members.

Now, if your determination to "get it more cheaply" has more to do with your bias that marketing is a necessary evil or a big crock, then by all means save the money and see how far it gets you. Some people need to learn the hard and expensive way. Others are just lucky.

TRUTH #10:

The money you spend on marketing is an investment and should be seen as such. Cheap investments often yield cheap results. Solid investments more often yield strong results.

The best way to save money and avoid spending more than you have to is to start early in the game. Good planning is worth its weight in gold. And there's no such thing as starting too soon for laying the foundation for your marketing program. Realistically, we know that in the heat of getting a company or product up and running, marketing is often assigned a back seat. We know that if you are reading this book, it may be too late to start early. That's all right. Let's go to plan B.

What can you do to jump-start your marketing program without indiscriminately throwing money at it? You have three options.

Option 1: Hire an experienced marketing manager who has a proven track record of launching products and companies in your industry and whose position is dedicated to marketing. The manager's experience and expertise will make him or her your in-house champion for, among other things, the positioning, strategies, and branding of your company. Then, the manager can contact less expensive vendors to generate the materials. As the guru, the manager will be responsible for making sure all the materials adhere to a single vision and are produced on time and on budget.

Because the in-house manager is on your staff, he or she can oversee all of your materials. Giving the manager responsibility for establishing and managing a budget means you have some assurances and control over the expenditure of marketing dollars. Other duties can include setting up trade shows, preparing presentations for investors, managing all PR efforts, and supporting salespeople.

Three requirements are necessary to make this scenario work. One, make sure you empower the manager to carry out his or her duties. Two, be available to make decisions. Three, make sure this person has the experience you need.

Option 2: Hire an experienced consultant who can set up the whole marketing scenario for you and then coach you through it. You will do the actual work. This solution is cost effective but will require a lot of your time and effort. It will also require you to locate vendors, learn about printing issues, interface with designers and writers, etc.

Option 3: Immediately shop for an established marketing agency, one that is not too big, does not have a minimum billing threshold, and is willing to work on a project-by-project basis or has a low retainer requirement. Make the first project a branding exploration that ends in a presentation of three possible paths that show what your marketing materials would look like and your messaging and tone. This will give you a global view of where marketing can take you. If you do not have a logo, make the branding exploration your second project and develop the logo first.

Conversely, when something fails in the company, everyone tends to point to marketing as the reason for the failure. In this case, examine your spending. How much did you spend? How soon did you spend it? What did you get for your money? What results did it produce? Quite possibly, for the money spent and the time allotted, the marketing was probably successful.

Check your strategy. Re-evaluate your media and your budget. Are you spending enough to get the right impact? Are your efforts directed to the right audience? Is the sales team following up on leads? What were your expectations and your strategic goals? Are you dealing with a product failure? Did the CEO have bigger expectations of the efforts or unrealistic expectations? Was your strategy not focused enough or targeted enough? Were you spending enough to make an impact?

Marketing failures are often indicative of a company's deeper problem. These problems can include the C-level management team, lack of support for the sales team or by the sales team, insufficient operations, or just stinginess or lack of understanding of the need for marketing and how to use it. Therefore, marketing becomes the fall guy.

CRITICAL TAKEAWAY: Marketing a new product or company is an ongoing process that is cumulative in its effects and syner-

gistic with other functions in the company, such as sales and operations. Getting the most value for your investment requires continual oversight and constant re-evaluation and nurturing.

Case History: Miami Rubber

Miami Rubber is a supplier of ready-to-install marine parts and offers one of the most extensive and comprehensive lineups of parts in its marketplace. Like many companies approaching their first web site, it chose to go with a cheap option. As you can see, the finished web site reflected this—an uncoordinated and unstrategic execution.

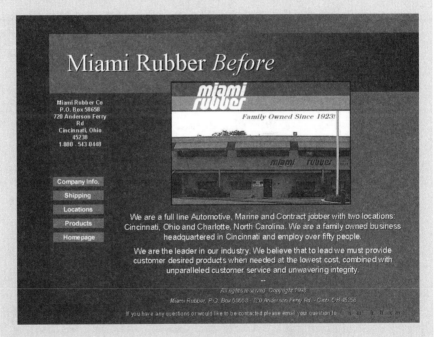

Miami Rubber *Before*

Miami Rubber Co
P.O. Box 58658
720 Anderson Ferry Rd.
Cincinnati, Ohio 45238
1-800-543-0448

Family Owned Since 1923!

Company Info.
Shipping
Locations
Products
Homepage

We are a full line Automotive, Marine and Contract jobber with two locations: Cincinnati, Ohio and Charlotte, North Carolina. We are a family owned business headquartered in Cincinnati and employ over fifty people.

We are the leader in our industry. We believe that to lead we must provide customer desired products when needed at the lowest cost, combined with unparalleled customer service and unwavering integrity.

--

All rights reserved. Copyright 1998
Miami Rubber, P.O. Box 58658 - 720 Anderson Ferry Rd - Cinti OH 45258

If you have any questions or would like to be contacted please email your question to

Though this web site did produce some results, its amateurish look reflected poorly on this well-established company for a number of reasons:

It was poorly designed. The logo is hidden in the picture and is hard to read. So it takes a minute to figure out the company name. The design is clunky and does not convey an image of a strong, successful company. The picture of the office is gratuitous, since the company's products are not dependent on the company's physical location or look. Its office building, though nice, does not deliver any message about size or substance. On first glance, the building looks like a car wash or strip mall. The photo would have served the company better had it been placed on the "About Us" page.

The text was poorly written. The body copy delivers no clear message about the company's considerable strengths. There is no message flow, and the style is static and boring.

You cannot immediately be sure of the company's business. No clear statement exists about what the company sells or why you should explore the web site further.

The company is not positioned. Neither the copy nor the graphics differentiate the company from its competition, though the company has a dramatic edge in the marketplace.

The web site provides extraneous information. That the company is family-owned is unimportant to the business. The two locations help establish size and convenience but are support statements and not immediate key points. The inclusion of what sounds like part of a mission statement is not the stuff that makes buyers stay on the web site. These are all points of corporate pride and interesting sidebars, but they get in the way of immediately convincing visitors that this web site is the right place to be.

When the company was ready to take its communications materials to the next level, it brought in professional marketing and creative help. Below is the result, which shows a big difference. Now, what works about this home page?

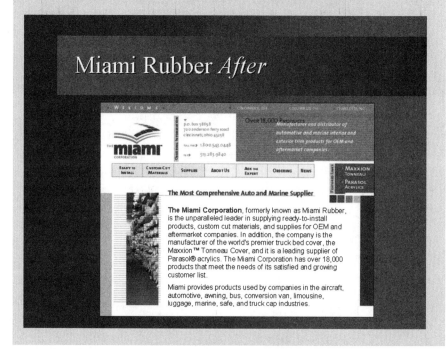

The professionals have rebranded the company. They developed a new name and logo, which is prominently displayed, and showed a communications platform that quickly informs potential buyers they have come to the right place.

The web site is carefully and professionally designed. Along with the company logo, copy platform, and other branding materials, the developed color palette maintains the look and feel of the web site and marries it to the other marketing materials.

It's well written. The copy now tells a compelling story that is benefit-driven. Contact information is immediately accessible.

The company has true claims that differentiate. The company has developed a unique selling proposition (USP), or differentiator, that highlights its extensive line of 18,000 parts. It also shows a superiority claim based on the differentiator, which is prominently placed on the home page. Sister companies also have differentiators.

The navigation is customer-focused. As you can see from the buttons, visitors can immediately locate the specific information they're seeking. This is critical to developing an effective web site. Accessible links to sister companies and branch offices increase the site's usefulness.

So, Can You Get the Work Done Cheaper?

Sometimes yes and sometimes no. Strategic advice and promotional help does not have to cost so much. Here are three things to keep in mind:

1. Is the cheaper work strategically thought out?

2. Are you being penny-wise and pound-foolish?

3. Be careful of "full service" agencies and other agencies with hidden costs (such as minimum billing thresholds).

Think twice before using friends and family. "I have relatives and neighbors (students) who can do this for me, and I will not have to pay for it." You always have to pay for it, if not in money then in time lost. Remember the old adage: There's never time/money to do it right, but there's always time/money to do it over.

You need to be able to separate your feelings for these people from making solid business decisions, and this is hard to do with relatives or friends. By judging each circumstance individually and dispassionately, you should be able to make the best price and value decision for your company.

No More Lies

Now that you have traveled through this book, we hope you have more than an inkling of the marketing process you need to go through to launch a product or company. You know what all the steps are, how to find the right people to help you, and how to spot your own marketing lies a mile away. More importantly, you know how to work your way through them.

You've learned that if you ignore these lies, they won't go away. However, your business might. It's our sincere hope that you've taken our truths, lessons, and shared experiences to heart and applied them to your own business. And we're looking forward to hearing your successful case histories.

Biographies of Those Quoted

Lie #1 — *Marv Goldschmitt*

Marv has over 25 years' experience helping to launch emerging technology companies. His work experience includes running the third oldest U.S. computer store and introducing Lotus 1-2-3 to the market as Lotus Development Corporation's first Head of Marketing. He also served as Lotus's first Vice President of Business Development, where he was responsible for the company's OEM strategy, international expansion, and industry relations. He has since served numerous technology startups as an executive, director, and consultant. He is currently Vice President of Tizor Systems, Inc., a network security company, and serves on several companies' boards of advisors.

Lie #2 — *Susan A. Harsley*

Susan is Vice President of Marketing for MFX, a leading provider of information technology for the insurance industry. Susan began her marketing career in 1996 with American International Group, Inc., where after ten years of various managerial positions in IT, she headed up the marketing area of AITE, the IT outsourcing division of AIG. In 2002, Susan was taken from AIG to write the business plan for MFX and lead the marketing efforts for this start-up IT company. Susan and MFX have been "moving at the speed of opportunity" ever since.

Lie #3 — *Scott E. Coleridge*

Scott has over 25 years' experience in the life sciences market. He has held executive positions in marketing, sales, and general management in various diagnostics, medical device, and biotechnology companies. He was CEO of the company that developed the first whole blood cholesterol test. In 2001, when he was CEO of

Synthon Chiragenics, his company won the New Jersey Technology Council's prestigious "Private Company of the Year" award. He also has 20 years' experience in women's healthcare, including minimally invasive gynecological surgery and contraception.

Lie #4 — Denise Drace-Brownell

Denise is an accomplished business executive whose unique background in law, finance, and technology distinguishes her as an effective strategist for difficult business and marketing challenges. Her clients have included several Fortune 500 companies, such as Akzo Nobel, Johnson & Johnson, and United Technologies, and numerous emerging companies, such as Myriad Genetics and The Medicines Company. While president of a brand strategy unit at McCann WorldGroup, she developed methodologies to identify and build corporate reputations. Her approach was used in the positioning of corporate restructurings, including the GlaxoSmithKline merger.

Lie #5 — Louis Gaburo

Louis has over 25 years' experience working with start-up companies, diagnostics, and technology licensing and commercialization. He has been Acting Director at the Enterprise Development Center at New Jersey Institute of Technology since 1997 and prior to that was Manager of the Technology Help Desk at the Rutgers University incubator. He was Director of Business Development and Licensing at Roche Diagnostic Systems, General Manager at Roche Analytical Systems (a medical device start-up), and a Marketing Manager of *in vitro* diagnostics for Roche Diagnostics. Louis was trained in biology and chemistry at Penn State and has an MS in biochemistry from Rutgers University and an MBA from Fairleigh Dickinson University.

Lie #6 — Christine Terashita

Christine is a marketing and communications professional with 20 years' experience in developing and executing integrated marketing and communications programs, with special expertise in start-up situations. She has worked in the publishing, advertising, investment, and technology sectors with companies such as MaRS Discovery District, BPI Capital Management (before it was bought by CI Funds Management), Investors Group, Transamerica Life, and *enRoute* and *Chatelaine* magazines. She has a bachelor's degree in Radio and Television Arts from Ryerson University, a bachelor's degree in Political Science and French from the University of Toronto, and an MBA from the Joseph L. Rotman School of Management, University of Toronto.

Lie #7 — Dennis J. Purcell

Dennis is Senior Managing Director of Aisling Capital LLC (formerly Perseus-Soros Biopharmaceutical Fund). He is currently responsible for the management of two funds that oversee $1 billion devoted to the biotechnology industry. Previous career activity included Managing Director of the Life Sciences Investment Banking Group at ChaseH&Q (formerly Hambrecht & Quist LLC) and Managing Director in the Healthcare Group at PaineWebber, Inc.

Lie #8 — Joan Rose

Joan applies her extensive branding and marketing experience in her position as Assistant Dean for Communications at Penn Law (University of Pennsylvania Law School). Previously, as a Senior Vice President at several advertising agencies, she helped launch new brands, sustain and reinvigorate brands in aging industries, worked with both high-tech and no-tech companies, and even enjoyed a stint as the Director of Advertising at the Sands Hotel & Casino in Atlantic City—giving her a unique perspective on launching and sustaining brands. Many of the projects garnered awards for their strategy and execution; more importantly, many of the companies and enterprises overcame their business challenges.

Lie #9 — Frank DeVito

Frank is a Partner in DeVito Fitterman Advertising and agency President. Prior to starting his own agency he was Vice Chairman, Chief Creative Officer of Lintas Worldwide, where he drove multinational business such as Coca-Cola, Johnson & Johnson, Unilever, Nabisco, Hanes, Winston, IBM, and MasterCard around the world. Prior to that he was Creative Director of Young & Rubicam NY. Along the way his work has won numerous marketing and creative awards. He has two sons, both in advertising, and showed signs of being a leader early on as a Captain, Infantry Company Commander, in the U.S. Army.

Lie #10 — Joe Bergmann

Joe has over 20 years of marketing and 16 years of interactive experience and has developed over 70 major Internet projects. He conceived and developed one of the first interactive marketing campaigns, which was for The Glenlivet Scotch. Some of his other clients have been American Express, Time Warner, Merrill Lynch, Hearst Publications, General Electric and Alliance Capital. At Holtzman Communications he has been an Internet Strategist, Creative Director, Information/Interaction Architect and writer. One of his innovations is how he conducts the discovery process. It's called OpenMind® Research. This unique approach has enabled many companies to be successful on the Web.

About the Authors

Sandra Holtzman founded Holtzman Communications, LLC in 1997. She has over 20 years of expertise in virtually every area of pharmaceutical advertising (ethical, OTC, DTC) in every medium and has worked in information technology, nanotech, chemical, emerging and converging technologies, consumer advertising (including the launch team of the Acura car), news, and the feature and industrial film business. Sandra is also the Co-Chair of the New York Chapter of the Licensing Executives Society; marketing columnist for *Lab to Wall Street,* a webzine focusing on biotechnology with C-level international readership (www.labtowallstreet.com); author of "Websites that Click" in the January 2005 issue of *Pharmaceutical Executive;* and author of a chapter on marketing in *A Comprehensive Guide to Business Incubation,* the top-selling book published by the National Business Incubation Association. She lectures about marketing and creating effective web sites, and sits on industry panels. Samples of her award-winning work can be found on her company's web site, www.holtzmancom.com. Her industry recognition includes Who's Who in Advertising and Who's Who in Media and Communications; Gold, Silver and Awards of Excellence from Advertising Women of New York; In Awe / Medical Marketing Association; International Advertising Festival of New York; New York Art Directors Club; New Jersey Art Directors Club; and Rx Club Show.

Jean Kondek heads up her own newly launched agency, Black Dog Marketing Services. She has over two decades of experience working as a strategic marketing executive and Creative Director / Copywriter in agencies such as Lintas, Y&R, McCann Erickson, BBDO, and Grey Advertising. During her time on Madison Avenue she worked on well-known national brands such as Nabisco, McNeil Labs, Advil, Dr. Pepper, Tampax, L'Oreal, 7-Eleven, Johnson & Johnson, Miller Beer, Old Milwaukee, AT&T, and Revlon. She has also worked in regional agencies, such as Princeton Communications Group, Inc., where her clients have included start-ups as well as established companies in the biotech, information technology, and healthcare markets, and on local businesses. She has won numerous awards including a Gold Lion from the Cannes Film Festival for commercials produced for 7-Eleven. Along the way she has taught marketing in community college and creative thinking at the School of Visual Arts in New York City. After hours, when not working on her fixer-upper, she can be found in a canoe on the Delaware River.